Chevy
Spotter's
Guide
1920-1980

TAD BURNESS

Motorbooks International
Publishers & Wholesalers Inc
Osceola, Wisconsin 54020, USA

© Tad Burness, 1981

ISBN: 0-87938-151-5

Library of Congress Catalog Card Number: 81-9477

Printed and bound in the United States of America

10 9 8 7 6 5 4 3 2

Motorbooks International books are also available at discounts in bulk quantity for industrial or sales-promotional use. For details write to Marketing Manager, Motorbooks International, P. O. Box 2, Osceola, Wisconsin 54020.

```
Library of Congress Cataloging in Publication Data

Burness, Tad, 1933-
    Chevy spotter's guide 1920-1980.

    1. Chevrolet automobile.   I. Title.
TL215.C5B87      629.2'222      81-9477
ISBN 0-87938-151-5 (pbk.)        AACR2
```

All material in this book is reprinted from the following volumes:

American Car Spotter's Guide 1920-1939, American Car Spotter's Guide 1940-1965, American Car Spotter's Guide 1966-1980 and *American Truck Spotter's Guide 1920-1970*.

Introduction

The familiar blue-and-white bow-tie emblem is known throughout the world, as Chevrolet's popularity continues. During most years since 1927, Chevy has managed to outsell even Ford. Thus, it's strange to learn that, in the early 1920's, General Motors Corporation was thinking of dropping this famous brand which has since become so profitable.

Chevrolet was founded during 1911 and joined the GM family in 1918. Its widespread popularity came after the mid-1920's, as Chevy offered luxuries not found in Ford's Model T: such as a sliding-gear transmission and more attractive styling. Also, GM maintained a strong advertising campaign. In 1929, Chevrolet introduced a smooth new six-cylinder engine, while Ford continued with four cylinders until 1932.

There are millions of loyal Chevy fans, and some have favorite year models among the older ones. The contents of this book have been reprinted from the Chevrolet sections of the complete American Car Spotter's Guides of 1920-1939, 1940-1965 and 1966-1980, as well as from the American Truck Spotter's Guide, 1920-1970.

I hope you will truly enjoy this new, special book for Chevy fans, and that it will give you much pleasant browsing and help you identify each year model on sight! You'll be happy to find the Corvette, Camaro, Corvair, Chevette and Chevy II Nova also included, as they are a part of Chevrolet's big family.

Tad Burness
Box 247
Pacific Grove, California
93950

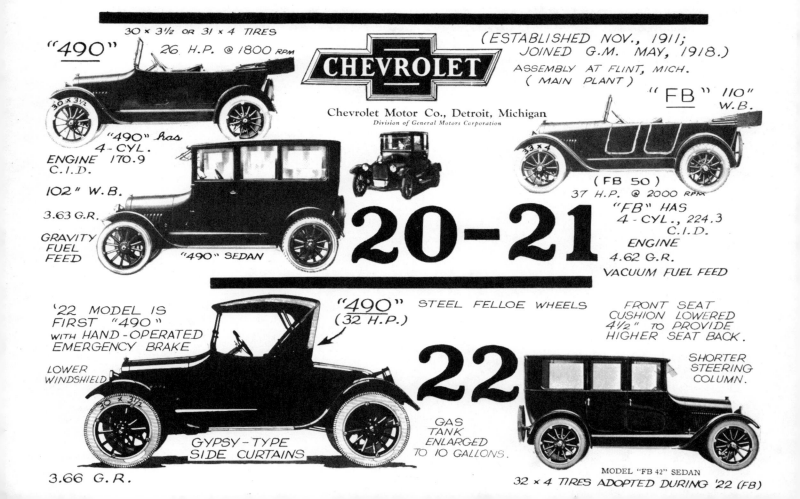

"490"

30 × 3½ or 31 × 4 TIRES

26 H.P. @ 1800 RPM

30 × 3¼

CHEVROLET

(ESTABLISHED NOV., 1911; JOINED G.M. MAY, 1918.)

ASSEMBLY AT FLINT, MICH. (MAIN PLANT)

Chevrolet Motor Co., Detroit, Michigan
Division of General Motors Corporation

"FB" 110" W.B.

33 × 4

"490" has
4-CYL.
ENGINE 170.9
C.I.D.

102" W.B.

3.63 G.R.

GRAVITY
FUEL
FEED

"490" SEDAN

20-21

(FB 50)
37 H.P. @ 2000 RPM

"FB" HAS
4-CYL., 224.3
C.I.D.
ENGINE
4.62 G.R.

VACUUM FUEL FEED

'22 MODEL IS
FIRST "490"
WITH HAND-OPERATED
EMERGENCY BRAKE

"490"
(32 H.P.)

STEEL FELLOE WHEELS

FRONT SEAT
CUSHION LOWERED
4½" TO PROVIDE
HIGHER SEAT BACK.

LOWER
WINDSHIELD

SHORTER
STEERING
COLUMN.

30 × 3½

22

GYPSY-TYPE
SIDE CURTAINS

GAS
TANK
ENLARGED
TO 10 GALLONS.

3.66 G.R.

MODEL "FB 42" SEDAN

32 × 4 TIRES ADOPTED DURING '22 (FB)

CHEVROLET

SUPERIOR" (B) (759 AIR-COOLED SERIES C, M CHEVROLETS ALSO BLT., JAN.,'23 TO MAY,'23. RECALLED BY FACTORY, JUNE '23. 4 CYL., 134.7 C.I.D., 4.44 G.R.)

WHEELBASE INCREASED TO 103" ON ALL.

23

1923 4-Passenger Sedanette

3.77 G.R. (THROUGH '24)

EARLY "B" TYPE (9-23 TO 1-24)

CURVED FRONT AXLE AND CABLE-OPERATED BRAKES.

24

"SUPERIOR" NAME CONT'D. THROUGH '26. (24½)

26 H.P. @ 2000 RPM (THROUGH '27)

FINAL YEAR WITH CONE CLUTCH

24½ DE LUXE (NICKEL TRIM)

LATER ("F") TYPE has STRAIGHT FRONT AXLE and BRAKE RODS.

29 x 4.40 BALLOON TIRES (CLOSED MODELS)

8-25: new KLAXON HORN, new STEER. WHEEL with CORRUGATED WALNUT FINISH RIM

I-PC. "VV" (VERTICAL VENTILATING) WINDSHIELD (ON CLOSED CARS.)

3.82 G.R. (THROUGH '31)

25

(K)

INTRO. I-3-25

NEW RADIATOR DESIGN

30 x 3½ TIRES ON OPEN MODELS

5

for Economical Transportation

CHEVROLET

26
(V)

NEW TIE-BAR BETWEEN HEADLIGHTS
29 × 4.40 TIRES (THROUGH '27)

AIR CLEANER INTRODUCED

(INTERIOR)

GENERATOR MOVED FROM RIGHT TO LEFT SIDE OF ENGINE ('26.)

FROM '23 TO '26, CHEVROLET CARS BLT. SEPT. OR LATER ARE SOMETIMES CLASSIFIED AS FOLLOWING YEAR'S MODEL, THOUGH ACTUAL MODEL CHANGE (DURING THESE YEARS) OCCURS IN JANUARY.

COACH HAS GREEN CORDUROY UPHOLSTERY.
SEDAN HAS BLUE CORDUROY.
BROWN "PLUSH" IN COUPE.

new SPARE TIRE CARRIER

('27½)

IMPERIAL LANDAU (INTRODUCED MAY, 1927)

TOURING CAR

CO-INCIDENTAL STEERING and IGNITION LOCK

new "BULLET" HEADLIGHTS

NEW RADIATOR DESIGN

27
(AA)
"CAPITOL"

new AC OIL FILTER, AC AIR CLEANER

ROADSTER

new 1-PC. FULL-CROWN FENDERS

for Economical Transportation

CHEVROLET

(FINAL 4-CYL. MODEL)

28

(AB)
"NATIONAL"

57376

Bigger and Better

HORSEPOWER INCREASED TO 35 @ 2200 RPM

WHEELBASE INCREASED TO 107"

NEW RADIATOR DESIGN AGAIN

4 - WHEEL BRAKES

for Economical Transportation

CHEVROLET

INTERIOR

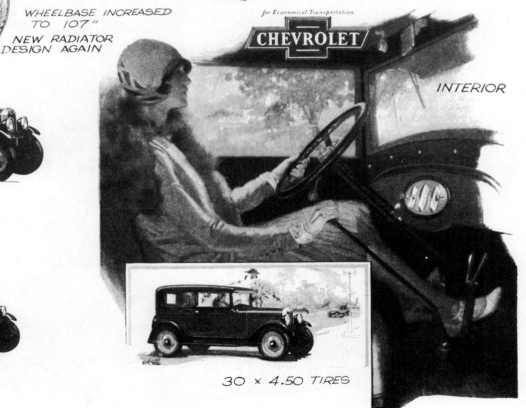

30 x 4.50 TIRES

NEW CHEVROLET SIX

(6-CYLINDER CHEVROLETS ONLY—1929 THROUGH 1954.)

ALL-NEW 1929 ENGINE →

193.9 C.I.D.

46 H.P. @ 2600 RPM

29

(AC) "INTERNATIONAL"

COMPLETELY RESTYLED

new FUEL PUMP

FISHER BODIES, AS BEFORE

CHEVROLET
for Economical Transportation

'29 DASH HAS 3 UPRIGHT OVALS WITHIN HORIZONTAL OVAL PANEL. ('30 DASH HAS SMALL CIRCULAR INSTRUMENTS.)

1929 IS FINAL CHEVROLET WITH FUEL GAUGE LOCATED OUTSIDE, ON TANK.

4.50 x 20" TIRES

3.81 G.R.—(ACCORDING TO CERTAIN SOURCES; 3.82 OTHERWISE.)

for Economical Transportation

CHEVROLET

30
"UNIVERSAL" (AD)

New Dash Gasoline Gauge

NEW DARK-FACED, CIRCULAR GAUGES

50 H.P. @ 2600 RPM

The Chevrolet Special Sedan is a de luxe creation in every sense of the word. Standard equipment includes six wire wheels with fender wells, bumpers front and rear, robe rail, dome light, silk assist cords, etc.

THE ROADSTER

THE SPORT ROADSTER

THE COUPE

THE SPORT COUPE

THE SEDAN

(CABRIOLET SUSPENDED FOR 1930; RE-INTRODUCED JANUARY, 1931.)

THE PHAETON

4.75 x 19" TIRES (THROUGH '31) AND NEW, SLIGHTLY SLANTED NON-GLARE WINDSHIELD →

THE CLUB SEDAN

(30 ½ MODEL HAS *Landau Irons*.)

THE COACH

9

CHEVROLET

31

NEW 109" WHEELBASE

STANDARD '31s DO NOT HAVE THE NEW RADIATOR STONE GUARD.

2 NEW BODY TYPES IN '31 →

(AE) "INDEPENDENCE"

THE STANDARD COACH

DASH ('31)

HORN BUTTON — OIL PRESSURE GAUGE — SPEEDOMETER — CHOKE BUTTON — THROTTLE GAUGE — GASOLINE GAUGE — AMMETER — WATER TEMPERATURE INDICATOR — SPARK BUTTON — LIGHTING SWITCH — GEARSHIFT LEVER — IGNITION LOCK — CLUTCH PEDAL — BRAKE PEDAL — HEAD LAMP DIMMER SWITCH — ACCELERATOR — STARTING PEDAL — HAND BRAKE LEVER — ACCELERATOR FOOT REST

'32 HAS NEW SYNCHRO-MESH TRANSMISSION

DASH ('32)

FREE WHEELING BUTTON — HORN BUTTON — OIL PRESSURE GAUGE — SPEEDOMETER — CHOKE BUTTON — HEAT CONTROL BUTTON — THROTTLE BUTTON — GASOLINE GAUGE — AMMETER — WATER TEMPERATURE — SPARK BUTTON — LIGHTING SWITCH — GEARSHIFT LEVER — IGNITION LOCK — CLUTCH PEDAL — BRAKE PEDAL — HEAD LAMP DIMMER SWITCH — ACCELERATOR — STARTING PEDAL — HAND BRAKE — ACCELERATOR FOOT REST

"CONFEDERATE" (BA)

32

60 H.P. @ 3000 RPM

"FREE WHEELING" (New)

4.1 G.R.

5.25 x 18" TIRES

THE SPORT ROADSTER

107" W.B.
4.3 GEAR RATIO

5.25 x 17" TIRES

CHEVROLET

33

MASTER and EAGLE "CA"

STARTS 12-32

206.8 C.I.D. 65 H.P. @ 2800 RPM

5.25 x 18" TIRES

181 C.I.D. 60 H.P. @ 3000 RPM

STANDARD "CC"
(WITH HOOD LOUVRES)
STARTS 3-33

DASH

(110" W.B.)
ACCELERATOR CONTROLS STARTER

4.11 GEAR RATIO (THROUGH '36)

NEW "KNEE ACTION" INDEPENDENT FRONT WHEEL SUSPENSION (WITH FRONT COIL SPRINGS) ON "MASTER" (DA) SERIES.

CHEVROLET MASTER SIX COUPE

CHEVROLET MASTER SIX SPORT COUPE

34

"STANDARD" (DC) SERIES INTRODUCED LATE (SPRING, 1934) WITH 107" W.B., 5.25 x 17" TIRES, 181 C.I.D. ENGINE WITH 60 H.P. @ 3000 RPM

"MASTER" HAS 112" W.B., 5.50 x 17" TIRES, 206.8 C.I.D. ENGINE WITH 80 H.P. @ 3300 RPM

DASH

11

CHEVROLET

"STANDARD" MODEL (EC) RESEMBLES 1934 BUT HAS PAINTED HEADLIGHT SHELLS. ← DASH GAUGES MOVED TO CENTER.

"MASTER" (EA and ED)

"ED" SERIES AVAIL. W/O "KNEE ACTION"

35

(ALL MODELS NOW HAVE THE 80-H.P. "BLUE FLAME" ENGINE.)

3-WINDOW SPORT COUPE WITH RUMBLE SEAT

(5-WINDOW BUSINESS COUPE ALSO AVAILABLE)   NEW 113" W.B. (MASTER) (STD. RETAINS 107" W.B.)

H.P. REDUCED TO 79 @ 3200 RPM, FOR '36

"EXPEDITER" COUPE AVAIL. WITH PICKUP BOX

(FC) STANDARD ═══ 109" W.B.
MASTER ═══ 113" W.B.
(FA and FD)
"KNEE ACTION" OPTIONAL (FA)

36

'36 DASH

NEW 216.5 C.I.D. 1937 ENGINE (85 H.P. @ 3200 RPM)

37

NEW STYLING ALSO

"GB" ═══ MASTER (3.73 G.R.)
"GA" ═══ MASTER DE LUXE WITH "KNEE ACTION" (4.22 G.R.)

112¼" W.B. ON ALL (THROUGH 1939)

6.00 × 16" IS NOW THE TIRE SIZE ON ALL MODELS.

'37 DASH

(1937 GEAR RATIOS
CONTINUED
THROUGH '39)

CHEVROLET

"HB" = MASTER
"HA" = MASTER DE LUXE

38

ASH TRAY IN
MASTER
DE LUXE
MODELS

'38 DASH

CHROME TRIM, GRILLE AND OUTSIDE DOOR HANDLES HAVE DECORATIVE
VERMILLION-RED STRIPES IN HORIZONTAL GROOVES.

"JB" = MASTER
"JA" = MASTER DE LUXE
85 H.P. @ 3200 RPM,
AS BEFORE.

FISHER BODIES, AS BEFORE

NEW STEERING COLUMN GEARSHIFT CONTROL
IS OPTIONAL. HAND BRAKE LEVER
HUNG AT LEFT,
BELOW DASH.

THE MASTER DE LUXE
FOUR-PASSENGER COUPE

39

'39
INTERIOR

13

CHEVROLET

(EST. 1911)
SINCE 1912
6 CYL.
(SINCE '29)

GM — BODY by FISHER

SPEC. DLX. DASH

MASTER 85 HAS STRAIGHT FRONT AXLE, OTHERS *have* "KNEE ACTION."

MINE FOR 1940

note LIGHTS PARTIALLY SUNK INTO FENDERS

COUPE

MASTER DE LUXE

new 113" WB

The Special De Luxe Sport Sedan, $802

COACH

new "BANNER" TYPE WIDE GRILLE

SEDAN

(MASTER 85 ENDS '40) MASTER DLX. *and* SPEC. DLX. ARE CONT'D. THROUGH '41

USA·1

Let This Power Cylinder Shift for You!

$659
MASTER 85 BUSINESS COUPE

Only Chevrolet has the New Exclusive Vacuum-Power Shift ··· the only steering column gearshift that does 80% of the work for you and requires only 20% driver effort!

KB, KH, KA
6.00 × 16 TIRES (SINCE '37)

40 (RESTYLED)

216.5 CID 85 HP @ 3200 RPM (SINCE '37)

CVT.

14

CHEVROLET

HEADLIGHTS SUNKEN FURTHER INTO FENDERS

INTERIOR

90 HP @ 3300 RPM

AG, AH
41

PARKING LIGHTS MOVED DOWN

new 116" WB (THROUGH '48)

COUPE

new 2-SPOKE STEERING WHEEL

USA 1941

90-H.P. ENGINE	YES	VACUUM-POWER SHIFT *at NO EXTRA COST*	YES	UNITIZED KNEE-ACTION	YES	ORIGINAL FISHER NO DRAFT VENTILATION	YES
CONCEALED SAFETY-STEPS	YES	BODY BY FISHER *with UNISTEEL TURRET TOP*	YES	BOX-GIRDER FRAME	YES	TIPTOE-MATIC CLUTCH	YES

"BLACKOUT" MODELS have PAINTED TRIM IN PLACE of CHROME.

BG, BH
42-45

FLEETMASTER (BH)

STYLEMASTER, FLEETMASTER, FLEETLINE ARE new MODEL NAMES (THROUGH '48)

PARK. LIGHTS in new GRILLE

U.S.A. NO. 1

'42 MEDALLION

new "FADEAWAY" FENDERS

CHEVROLET

1942

CAR RATIONING RULES

recently announced by O.P.A. now make it much easier for eligible buyers to get delivery of new Chevrolets

(AS OF JUNE, 1942)

FLEETLINE MODELS ON NEXT PAGE

15

CHEVROLET

$880.

NEW CHEVROLET *Fleetline* AEROSEDAN

2 *New* "FLEETLINE" (BH) MODELS
EASILY IDENTIFIED BY 3 HORIZONTAL CHROME STRIPS ON EACH FENDER (THROUGH '48)

42-45 (CONT'D.)

NEW CHEVROLET *Fleetline* SPORTMASTER

SLOGAN: "THE FINEST CHEVROLET OF ALL TIME"

$920.

DK "FLEETMASTER" has CHROME TRIM AROUND WINDOW MOULDINGS

PRICE RANGE: $1022. TO $1614.

DJ, DK **46** new GRILLE

$1194. SPORT SEDAN

DJ "STYLEMASTER" (NO CHROME ON WINDOW or WINDSHIELD MOULDINGS.)

'46 MEDALLION

STYLEMASTER

CHEVROLET

$1255.

216.5 CID
90 HP @ 3300 RPM

116" WB

EK FLEETMASTER

new GRILLE has PROTRUDING CENTER SECTION

EJ, EK

47

$1775.

FLEETMASTER CVT.

new MEDALLION

EK FLEETLINE AERO

$1525.

EK FLEETLINE SPORTMASTER

FJ STYLEMASTER

FK 1948 CHEVROLET "FLEETMASTER" Four Door Sedan

$1340.

FJ, FK

48

new "T"-SHAPED PIECE ADDED AT CENTER OF GRILLE

FK FLEETLINE

AERO

PRICE RANGE: $1160. TO $1890.

PACE CAR AT 1948 INDY 500 RACE

17

CHEVROLET

FLEETLINE

2-DR.

4-DR.

METAL-BODIED WAGON

PRICES START AT **$1339.**

GJ = SPECIAL
GK = DE LUXE

GJ, GK
49
TOTALLY RESTYLED

1949 TRUNK LID has SMALL "T" HANDLE WHICH TURNS.

2-DR. TOWN SEDAN

4-DR. SPORT SEDAN

STYLELINE

SPORT CPE.

VERTICAL PIECES in LOWER HALF of GRILLE

new SHORTER 115" WB (THROUGH '57)

1949 HUBCAP has RED CENTER.

6.70 × 15

PONTOON-STYLE REAR FENDERS

all-new INTERIOR (LEFT AND RIGHT VIEWS)

DLX. MODELS have CHROME AROUND WINDOWS and on FRONT FENDERS

CHROME (DLX.)
BLACK RUBBER (SPEC.)

18

CHEVROLET

$1741.

new "Bel-Air" 2-DR. HARDTOP has WIDE BACKLIGHT →

DASH

1950 TRUNK LID has new RE-DESIGNED HANDLE.

STYLING SIMILAR TO 1949, EXCEPT FOR MINOR DIFFERENCES AS NOTED.

new AUTOMATIC TRANSMISSION AVAILABLE

HJ, HK

50

HJ = SPECIAL
HK = DE LUXE

new 1950 GRILLE WITHOUT VERTICAL LOWER CENTER PCS. SEEN IN '49.

PRICE RANGE: $1329. TO $1994.

First low-priced car with **POWERGlide** No-Shift driving *

* = POWERGLIDE SOMEWHAT LIKE BUICK'S "DYNAFLOW." (NOT INCLUDED IN ABOVE PRICES)

BACK SEAT (4-DR.)

The Styleline De Luxe 2-Door Sedan

1950 HUBCAP has YELLOW CENTER.

CHEVROLET

BEL-AIR $1914.

FLEETLINE

STYLELINE
DE LUXE

STYLELINE
PRICES START AT
$1460.

JJ, JK
51
GRILLE
CHANGED

DE LUXE

NEW Safety-Sight
Instrument Panel

INTERIOR
VIEWS

NEW Modern-Mode
Interiors

STYLELINE
DE LUXE

new CHROME TRIM STYLE.

CHEVROLET

NEW

26 Exterior Colors and two-tone color combinations to choose from.

New Softer, Smoother Ride with new and improved shock absorber action.

Improved Carburetion with Automatic Choke in Powerglide models.

New Centerpoise Power is smoother — "screens out" engine vibration.

Color-Matched Two-Tone Interiors bring new beauty to De Luxe models.

52
KJ, KK

$1696.

STYLELINE SPECIAL (has MINIMUM of CHROME TRIM)

FLEETLINE DLX. (NO MORE FLEETLN. SPECIAL)

STYLELINE DE LUXE 2-DR.

new 5 RIDGES RUN DOWN CENTER HORIZ. MEMBER of GRILLE.

new MEDALLION

STYLELINE DE LUXE SPORT COUPE (ABOVE)

$1519. TO $2281. PRICE RANGE

(2 VIEWS)

$1992.

BEL AIR (IN STYLELINE DLX. SERIES) H/T

FINAL YEAR FOR STYLELINE and FLEETLINE MODEL NAMES.

CHEVROLET

150

AT RIGHT: 210 SEDAN
(IN SAN FRANCISCO, CALIF.) →

210
2-DR.

BEL AIR SEDAN
(INTERIOR)

53
(TOTALLY
RESTYLED)

"Handyman"
(two of them)   6-PASS.

150
station wagons

210

BEL AIR
(note
EXTRA
TRIM and
CONTRASTING
COLOR STRIP on
REAR FENDER.)

BEL AIR now
TOP-OF-LINE SERIES
WHICH INCLUDES 2-DR. SEDAN,
4-DR. SEDAN, CONVERTIBLE (ILLUSTRATED)
and H/T SPORT COUPE (ILLUSTRATED)

235 CID ENGINE
(THROUGH '62, ON 6-CYL.)
108 OR 115 HP @ 3600 RPM)

WITH IMITATION
WOODGRAIN
TRIM

Townsman   8-PASS.

CORVETTE
Sports Car by CHEVROLET
53

6- CYL. CHEVROLET ENGINE (TO '55)

STARTS 1953
$3512.

FIBERGLASS BODIES (ON ALL)

('54)

SPEAR ON SIDE EMBLEM NOW POINTS UP.

54-55

ILLUSTRATED with DETACHABLE TOP

FULL-LENGTH SIDE TRIM

V-8 ENGINE ALSO (1955)

PRICE CUT 1955   ('55)

new TOP

56-57

new SIDE TRIM

V-8s ONLY

$2900. ('56)

$3437. ('57)

4 HEADLIGHTS

102" WB
230 HP

DASH

58

new VENT LOUVRE GROUP ON TOP OF HOOD (1958 ONLY)

$3631.

new BUMPERS

59-60

$3872.
(IN '60 ; $3 LESS THAN '59)

CHEVROLET

new MEDALLION
new TAIL-LIGHTS

54

Push Button
Window Controls*

Toe-Touch Power
Brake Pedal*

Extra-Easy Power
Steering*

Powerglide
Automatic
Transmission*

Push Button
Door Latches

Push Lever
Heater Controls*

Push Button
Door Locks
(Keyless Locking)

Push Button
Radio Controls*

Automatic
Dome Light
Switches†

Push Button Glove
Compartment Lock
(Automatic Light†)

Pull Knob
Light Switch

Finger-Touch Horn
Blowing Ring†

Pull Knob
Ventilation
Controls

Key-Turn Starter
(Automatic Choke)

Turn Knob Wind-
shield Wiper Control
(Push Button Washer)*

Toe-Touch
Accelerator Treadle

Push Button
Headlight Dimmer

Lever Action Direction
Signal Control (Automatic Return)*

Push Button Automatic
Seat Adjustment Control*

Advanced Chevrolet Engineering brings

CYBERNETIC CHEVROLET
(Cybernetic = Automatic Control)

210 DELRAY COUPE

BEL
AIR

115 HP @ 3700 RPM
OR 125 HP @ 4000 RPM

new
OBLONG PARK. LIGHTS

new GRILLE *has* 5 VERTICAL PCS.
INSTEAD OF 3

24

150

$1593.

CHEVROLET

"ONE-FIFTY" HANDYMAN

2 VIEWS OF DASH

210 HANDYMAN

BEL AIR

THE "TWO-TEN" 4-DOOR SEDAN in Skyline Blue.

(TOTALLY RESTYLED)

new V-8

55

210 "TOWNSMAN" WAGON

ALSO AVAIL. (265 CID, 162 HP @ 4400 RPM
or 180 HP @ 4600 RPM)
6 CYL. has 123 HP @ 3800
or 136 HP @ 4200 RPM)

THE BEL AIR BEAUVILLE

new "NOMAD" 2-DR. WAGON

(CHROME STRIPS RUNNING DOWN TAILGATE.)

CVT. IS PACE CAR AT 1955 INDY 500 RACE

$2472. (6)

25

CHEVROLET

56

THE "ONE-FIFTY" HANDYMAN
2 doors, 6 passengers, versatile and thrifty..

THE "TWO-TEN" HANDYMAN
2 doors, 6 passengers, all-vinyl interior.

THE "TWO-TEN" BEAUVILLE
4 doors, 9 passengers.

THE "TWO-TEN" TOWNSMAN
4 doors, 6 passengers, loads of cargo space.

BEL AIR 4-DOOR HARDTOP and interior

AIR COND. DETAIL

Now in the low price field...

$2329.

AIR CONDITIONING!

All components are located "up front" ... out of sight and out of the way! Harrison air conditioning is available on four great GM cars—Chevrolet, Pontiac, Oldsmobile and Buick.

BEL AIR BEAUVILLE 9-PASS. WAGON

new SMALL ROUND LENSES IN TAIL-LIGHTS

210

CORVETTE

6.70 x 15 TIRES

BEL AIR SEDAN
140, 162, 170, 205 OR 225 HP

NOMAD

new FULL-WIDTH GRILLE

BEL AIR 2-DR.

CHEVROLET

PRICES START AT $1885.

150

new 7.50 × 14 TIRES

210

BEL AIR

1957 IS 3RD AND FINAL YEAR THAT THE NOMAD IS A SUPER-DELUXE 2-DOOR SPORT WAGON.

$2757. (6)

NEW TRIPLE-TURBINE TURBOGLIDE*

It's the last word in automatic drives. Super-smooth—and there's even a HILL RETARDER position on the selector, for safer control on the steepest down grades!

57

NOMAD and BEL AIR have new ANODIZED REAR FENDER PANEL.

4-DOOR WAGON

2-DR. H/T

BEL AIR

new GRILLE COMBINED with BUMPER

COMMAND POST CONTROL PANEL

HEADLIGHT-HOOD AIR VENTS

$2464.

4-DR. H/T

140, 162, 185, 220, 245, 250, 270 OR 283 HP (new 283 CID V8 JOINS 265 CID)

27

CHEVROLET

NOMAD
6-PASS.
4-DR.

DASH

BEL
AIR

4-DR., 6 OR 9-PASS.
BROOKWOOD

new 117½" WB
(1958 ONLY)

58

2-DR.
6-PASS.
YEOMAN

new
IMPALA

$2693.

new
WAGON TAILGATE

BISCAYNE

235 CID 6
has 145 HP
@ 4200
RPM

CROSS-
SECTION
OF "TURBO
THRUST"
V8 ENGINE

283 OR 348 CID V8s
(TO '62) (185 TO
280 HP)

IMPALAS
have 6
REAR LIGHTS,
AND EXTRA
"AIR SCOOP"
DECORATIONS.

CHEVROLET

1—*Biscayne Utility Sedan.* Chevy's prices start right here—a handy, handsome 2-door with 31 cu. ft. of cargo space behind front seat.

2—*Brookwood 2-Door,* Chevrolet's lowest priced wagon, is as dutiful as it is beautiful. Seats 6, holds up to 92 cu. ft. of cargo.

3—*Impala 4-Door,* most elegant family sedan in the line, makes you wonder why anyone would want a car that costs more.

4—*El Camino* combines stunning passenger car styling with the load space of a pickup. Good looks never carried so much weight!

5—*Impala Convertible.* Chevy's got a special formula for carefree top-down fun.

6—*Biscayne 2-Door.* This beauty's the lowest priced 6-passenger Chevy you can buy!

7—*Nomad 4-Door,* 6-passenger station wagon—finest of Chevrolet's 5 wonderful wagons.

8—*Bel Air 4-Door.* As luxurious as it looks, yet priced just above Chevy's thriftiest sedans.

9—*Brookwood 4-Door.* Chevy's lowest priced 4-door wagon seats 6, holds 92 cu. ft. of cargo with rear seat down.

10—*Bel Air 2-Door,* distinctively styled inside and out, carries a price tag just a notch above Chevy's thriftiest 2-door sedan.

11—*Impala Sport Sedan.* Here's a 4-door hardtop with the kind of looks and luxury you'd expect only on the most expensive makes.

12—*Kingswood 4-Door,* 9-passenger station wagon, offers rear-facing third seat and power-operated rear window at no extra cost.

13—*Impala Sport Coupe.* It's one of Chevy's full series of elegant Impalas for '59. And you won't find a handsomer hardtop anywhere!

14—*Parkwood 4-Door,* 6-passenger station wagon, distinctively trimmed inside and out, priced a shade above the thrifty Brookwoods.

15—*Bel Air Sport Sedan.* It's Chevy's lowest priced hardtop—and it makes beautiful sense!

16—*Corvette.* Take the wheel of America's only authentic sports car and treat yourself to the snappiest, happiest driving you've known.

17—*Biscayne 4-Door,* thriftiest 4-door sedan in the line, is another big reason

BROOKWOOD

135 TO 315 HP

PRICE RANGE $2160. TO $3009.

BEL AIR

NOMAD 4-DR., 6-PASS.

HUGE *new* TAIL-LIGHTS

59

(TOTALLY RESTYLED)

new 119" WB (THROUGH '70)

BIG "GULL WING" REAR DECK

IMPALA SPORT COUPE (H/T)

CHEVROLET

BISCAYNE

NOMAD

KINGSWOOD

60

PRICE RANGE: $2230. TO $2996.

BEL AIR

BEL AIR

new GRILLE

IMPALA SPORT CPE.

Impala 4-Door Sport Sedan

135 TO 335 HP

MODIFIED "GULL-WING" REAR STYLING, *with* *new* ROUND TAIL-LIGHTS

corvair

DASH

569 SEDAN

500
(NO CHROME BELT TRIM)

WITH THE ENGINE IN THE REAR

AIR-COOLED 6-CYL.
REAR ENGINE-TRANSAXLE UNIT
140 CID
80 HP @ 4400 RPM
6.50 x 13
TIRES 108" WB

60

GENERAL MOTORS
(1960 - 1969)
COMPACT CAR
by Chevrolet

$1984. and up

CLUB COUPE and INTERIOR (727)

700

SEDAN

$2103.
(769 SEDAN)

BACK SEAT FOLDS, FOR CARGO.

DWD 192

CHEVROLET

BROOKWOOD

BISCAYNE

135 TO 360 HP

NOMAD

new ROOFLINE
(SPT. CPE.)

BEL AIR

new ROOFLINE →

BEL AIR
SPT. SED.

IMPALA
(RESTYLED)

61

$2230.
TO $3099.

PRICE RANGE

(HT)
SPT.
CPE.

IMPALA

DASH

LIGHT CONTROL
SWITCH

CIGARETTE LIGHTER
AND ASH TRAY

RADIO CONTROLS

LEFT VENT
CONTROL

WIPER AND WASHER
CONTROL

HEATER
CONTROLS

RIGHT VENT
CONTROL

IGNITION
SWITCH

GLOVE BOX
AND LOCK

32

corvair

500

CLUB COUPE

spunkier 145-cu.-in. air-cooled rear engine

700

700 INTERIOR →

4-DOOR SEDANS

new OPTION. ELECTRIC HOT AIR HEATER

note UNIQUE WHEEL COVERS ON NEW MONZA →

new CORVAIR MONZA CLUB COUPE and INTERIOR →

61

2 new WAGON TYPES and 2 SUB-TYPES

CORVAIR GREENBRIER SPORTS WAGON

SWINGING SIDE DOORS 95" WB

$2651.

GREENBRIER (STD.)

$2331.

LAKEWOOD 500 (535)

LAKEWOOD STATION WAGONS

700 (735)

SMART, DURABLE INTERIORS—Shown here: the 700's rich fabric-vinyl upholstery, offered in three color-keyed choices. 500 all-vinyl interior also comes in three color-keyed blends. Check the push-button locks on rear doors. ▼

700

ENGINE UNDER REAR FLOOR.

33

CORVETTE $4272. **61**

new GRILLE

new 250 HP

$4375. **62** new SIDE-SCOOP DESIGN

63 new "STINGRAY"

$4589.

new SIDE-SCOOPS AGAIN

new GRILLE, CONCEALED HEADLIGHTS, new 98" WB

new 1-PC. BACKLIGHT →

64

Corvette Sting Ray Convertible in Saddle Tan

Corvette Sting Ray Sport Coupe in Riverside Red

$4627.

$4723.

327 CID V-8 has 250, 300, 350, 365 or 375 HP @ 5500 RPM

65 $4508.

4-WHEEL DISC BRAKES

new VERTICAL LOUVRE DESIGN

425 HP 396 CID V8 →

1965½ CORVETTE "396"

34

BISCAYNE

CHEVROLET

FINAL 235 CID 6 has 135 HP @ 4000 RPM

DASH

BEL AIR SPT. CPE. ROOFLINE

BEL AIR

1962

new GRILLE

IMPALA

283, new 327 OR new 409 CID V8s (170 TO 409 HP)

M-1042

IMPALA has ALUMINIZED PANELING AROUND TAIL-LIGHTS

OUTER-EDGE TAIL-LTS. DO NOT OPEN WITH TRUNK.

IMPALA

62

(IMPALA I.D.)

JET-SMOOTH RIDE

35

100

Chevy II 4 or 6 CYL. 110" WB

300

300

COMPACT CAR
by Chevrolet

(STARTS 1962)

REAR DETAILS

Nova

WAGON

Wagon

6.50 × 13 TIRES
ON
WAG.,
6.00 × 13
ON OTHERS

CONVERTIBLE
(SHOWING DASH,
INTERIOR DETAIL)

NOVA 400

POWER STEERING AVAIL.

PRICE RANGE:
62
$2051. TO $2793.

REAR and FRONT FENDER
and WHEEL COVER
DETAIL (NOVA 400)

DASH

(AS SEEN
FROM REAR
OF WAGON)

36

corvair

500

GREENBRIER

62

MONZA

MONZA WAGON (ABOVE)
(FINAL YEAR FOR THIS
"LAKEWOOD" STYLE WAGON.
GREENBRIER VAN-TYPE
WAGON AVAIL. THROUGH
1965.)

DASH (ALL BUT SPYDER)

new
CORVAIR SPYDER
(150 HP)

63

MONZA

BISCAYNE

DASH

IMPALA SPORT SEDAN

BEL AIR

new 230 CID 6 (140 HP @ 4400 RPM.

PRICE RANGE: **63** $2558. TO $3417.

IMPALA

note CONVERTIBLE-STYLE "CREASES" STAMPED INTO STEEL ROOF of THIS IMPALA SPORT COUPE.

V8s have 195 HP @ 4800 TO 425 HP @ 6000

new DIP IN MIDDLE OF DECK LID ON 1963 MODELS.

CHEVY II

100

$2313.

300

$2395.

$2710.

63

NOVA 400

CHEVY II NOVA 400 SUPER SPORT CONVERTIBLE

new GRILLE

120 HP
(6 CYL.)
(SINCE '62)

NEW V8 POWER
(OPTIONAL)

4, 6, OR V8

64

MORE '64s ON NEXT PAGE

1964 JET-SMOOTH CHEVROLET

BISCAYNE

BISCAYNE

BISCAYNE

new STRAIGHT-ACROSS DECK LID *with* CENTER RIDGE

2-DR. BISCAYNE $2590.,

BEL AIR

64

283, 327, 409 CID V8 ENGINES, SAME SIZES AS IN '63   6 = 140 HP
V8s = 195, 250, 300, 340, 400 OR 425 HP

3.08 TO 4.56 GEAR RATIOS

SPT. SEDAN 4-DR. H/T

9-PASS. WAGON

IMPALA

H/T

IMPALA SS

new IMPALA SS $3185.,

ONE OF VARIOUS 1964 UPHOLSTERY PATTERNS

new GRILLE

DASH

40

CHEVY II

INTERIOR

64
(CONT'D.)

SPT. CPE.

NOVA SS
(has THIS EMBLEM)

MA-5282

NOVA

CHEVY II

SEDAN

Super Sport

(TAILGATE OPEN)

NOVA

EC 4434

AAJ 030

(TAILGATE CLOSED,

SOLD

AO 4124

65

CHEVY II

SEE ALSO: Chevrolet

41

corvair

STD. ENGINE RAISED TO 95 HP.

DASH

64

MONZA

MONZA SPYDER (ABOVE) has 150 HP.

$3008.
(667 CVT.)

500

←DASH has CIRCULAR GAUGES.

MONZA

This year, all the coupes and sedans have hardtop styling

FROM $2281. **65**

new LARGER BODIES

(ONLY MAJOR CORVAIR RESTYLING)

New power choices, too. There's a new 140-hp engine that's standard in Corsa models and can be ordered for all others—and a 180-hp power plant that you can specify for your Corsa.

MONZA SPORT SEDAN

140 HP (CORSA IS NEW TOP OF LINE MODEL.)

CHEVELLE (NEW) by Chevrolet

(2-DR. WAGON ALSO AVAIL.)

194 OR 230 CID 6 (120 OR 155 HP @ 4400 RPM)

64

ALSO 283 CID V8 (195 OR 220 HP @ 4800 RPM)

INTERIOR (MALIBU)

300

MALIBU →

115" W.B.

CHEVELLE

300 DELUXE

300 2-DR.

300 2-DR. 6-PASS. WAGON (MALIBU 4-DR. WAGON has CHROME STRIP ALONG SIDE.)

MALIBU SS

new HORIZONTALLY-SPLIT GRILLE

65

MALIBU SS

194 OR 230 CID 6 (120 OR 140 HP @ 4400 RPM)
ALSO :
(283 CID V8 AVAIL. ONLY WITH 195 HP @ 4800 RPM)
3 new 327 CID V8s (250, 300, OR 350 HP)

43

CHEVROLET

$2669.. 4 DOOR BISCAYNE

7.35 x 14 TIRES

BEL AIR

1965

IMPALA

IMPALA 3-SEAT WAGON

$3444..

8.25 x 14 TIRES ON WAGONS

IMPALA DASH

LIGHTS
VENT
WIPER WASHER
IGNITION SWITCH
LIGHTER
ASH TRAY
RADIO
HEATER
GLOVE BOX
VENT

POPULARLY REFERRED TO AS THE "COKE BOTTLE" PROFILE

H/T

IMPALA SUPER SPORT

65 (TOTALLY RESTYLED) AVAIL. with VINYL TOP

with SPORT WHEEL COVERS →

← $3210..

SINCE 1918, MFD. BY **General Motors**

CHEVROLET

(EST. 1911) FROM $2832. (BISCAYNE 2-DR.)

Caprice DASH

IMPALA HUB CAP

IMPALA

66

new GRILLE, BUMPER and TAIL-LIGHT

(INTRO. THURSDAY 10-7-65)

119" WB
7.75/8.25
× 14 TIRES

STD. ENGINES
250 CID 6 (155 HP)
283 CID V8 (195 HP)

NEW

REAR VIEW

Caprice Custom Wagon

$3800.
(3-SEAT)

* CAPRICE

Custom Series

note HORIZONTAL BANDS ACROSS CAPRICE TAILLIGHTS (UNLIKE TAILLIGHTS OF BISCAYNE, BEL AIR or IMPALA MODELS)

CUSTOM SEDAN $3516.

*-(CAPRICE INTRO. 1965, AS A $242 OPT. PKG.)

$3453.
CAPR. CUST. CPE. ROOFLINE
(New)

DENOTES A 327 CID V8

45

CHEVELLE BY CHEVROLET

(SINCE 1964)

MID-SIZE

FULL COIL SUSPENSION

115" WB

(300 IS LOWEST-PRICED, LITTLE CHROME, $2607 UP. 300 DLX. has CHROME STRIP ALONG SIDE.)

MALIBU CVT. = $3030.

Malibu Wagon
2-SEAT

$3093.

MALIBU

H/T SPT. CPE.
$2821.

194 CID 6 (120 HP)
230 CID 6 (140 HP)
283 CID TURBO-FIRE V8
(195 OR 220 HP)
327 CID V8 (275 HP)
396 CID V8s
(325 OR 360 HP)

66

FLUSH-AND-DRY ROCKER PANELS

(300 TYPES have PLAINER REAR DECKS WITHOUT CHROME ORNAMENTATION)

DASH

OPTIONAL TACH. ←

SS 396 $3219.

SS has
Turbo-Jet V8's
(396 CID)

6.95/7.35 ×14 TIRES
(OPT. RED-STRIPE NYLON TIRE and MAG.-STYLE WHEEL COVER)

(SS CVT. ALSO AVAIL.)

(1962-1979) CHEVY II by CHEVROLET

DELUXE MODELS KNOWN AS

Nova

Station Wagon

153 CID 4 (93 HP)
194 CID 6 (120 HP)
283 CID V8 (195 HP)
6.50 × 13 TIRES
(WAG. = 6.95 × 14)

110" WB
(1962-1967)

66
new GRILLE;
new TALLER
TAIL-LTS.

NOVA H/
SUPER SPORT H/T
$2652.

LOWEST-PRICED
"100" 2-DR. IS $2250.)

STATION WAGON AVAIL. THROUGH '67.
(FROM $2709.)

NOVA SS
H/T
$2708.

4-CYL = 90 HP
6-CYL = 140 HP
V8 = 195 HP

67

1967 GRILLE
DIFFERENCE
ILLUSTR. AT
LOWER
LEFT

NOVA
4-DR.
$2519.

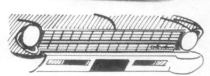

'67 Chevy II
The stylish economy car

47

(1960-1969)
MONZA

CHEVROLET CORVAIR

rear-engine design with
Independent suspension at all four wheels

A most unusual car for people who enjoy the unusual!

H/T $2556.

$2630.
SPT. SEDAN
(4-DR. H/T)

MONZA
CVT.
$2699.

(FINAL)
CORSA
$2666.
(H/T)

66
$2809.

1966
SALES:
88,951
("500" IS
LOWEST-PRICED
MODEL, FROM
$2289.)

| 108" WB | 6 CYL., 164 CID |
| 7.00 x 13 TIRES | 95-140 HP |

CORSA
SERIES
NO LONGER
AVAILABLE 1967

1967 SALES:
24,736

500

$2339.

67

New oval steering wheel—This easy-to-grip wheel sits atop the GM-developed energy-absorbing steering column—one of many new standard safety features. Others include 4-way hazard warning flasher and a lane-change feature incorporated in direction signal control.

THIS
BEST
IDENTIFIES
A 1967
MODEL.

95
OR
110 HP
ENGINES
ONLY,
DURING
1967.

MONZA CVT. $2770.

'67 Corvair
The rear-engine road car

48

Chevrolet

CORVETTE (SINCE 1953)

STINGRAY CPE.

* 98" WB (ALL) V8 ENGINES

OPT. 427 CID (425 HP)
STD. 327 CID (300 HP)

66-67

7.75 x 14 TIRES

('66) $4784.

FR. $4573.

FR. $4604.

(CVT. and H/T CVT. ALSO)

(* - SINCE 1963)

(TOTALLY RESTYLED)

327 CID (300 - 350 HP) OR 427 CID (390, 400 OR 435 HP)

68

OPT. HARD TOP ↓

$5157. CPE.

new F70 x 15 TIRES

CVT. $4814.

new T-TOP (INTERIOR)

Corvette simulated wood steering wheel and instrumentation.

49

CHEVELLE

$3079.

MALIBU

7.35 x 14 TIRES

H/T $2877.

DASH and CONSOLE

new GRILLES and TAIL-LIGHTS

Turbo-Jet V8

67 SS 396

new safety features standard — GM-developed energy-absorbing steering column, four-way hazard warning flasher, dual master cylinder brake system with warning light, folding front seat back latches.

SS 396.

H/T $3083.

SS 396

(F 70 x 14 TIRES ON SS-396)

SS 396

note "SS 396" IN GRILLE CENTER

2-SEAT CONCOURS

new TOP-OF-LINE WAGON (300 DLX. and MALIBU WAGONS ALSO AVAIL.)

$3269.

CHEVROLET Camaro (1967-1981)
(INTRO. 9-29-66)

6 CYL. OR V8
(140 TO 325 HP)
108" WB

NEW

STOCK CAMARO 6 COUPE (FROM $2792.)

RS (RALLY SPORT) WITH CONCEALED HEADLTS. AVAIL.

SS-350 CPE.
W. CONCEALED LTS.

67

"SS 350" ON GRILLE

SS - 350
WITH 350 CID V-8 ENG.
(295 HP) OR 396 CID (325 HP)

SS-350 Interior

Command Performance "The Hugger"

51

'67 Chevrolet gives you that sure feeling

Biscayne $3036.

$3469. UP

(INTRO. 9-29 66)

Impala

STANDARD
ENGINES
155-hp Turbo-Thrift 250 Six
195-hp Turbo-Fire 283 V8
EXTRA-COST
OPTIONAL ENGINES
275-hp Turbo-Fire 327 V8
325-hp Turbo-Jet 396 V8
385-hp Turbo-Jet 427 V8

'67 IMPALA

Impala SS $3350.

67 new GRILLE

$3192.

Caprice Custom Sedan

$3477.

1967

Impala Sport Coupe

new GRILLE IS HORIZONTALLY BISECTED BY BUMPER CROSS BAR

new ROUND TAIL LTS. IN BUMPER

CUSTOM CPE.

68

$3809. UP

CAPRICE

CUSTOM SEDAN $3621.

STD. 250 CID 6 (155 HP)
307 CID V8 (200 HP)

formal

$3371.

Impala coupes

note SMALL new SIDE LIGHTS

1968

Fastback SPORT CPE. $3318.

(INTRO. 9-21-67)

52

BE SMART! BE SURE! BUY NOW AT YOUR CHEVROLET DEALER'S.

DASH

Chevy II **NOVA**: The not-too-small car CHEVROLET

(WAGONS NO LONGER AVAIL.)

STD. 4-DR. (w/o SIDE CHROME)

SS

68

(TOTALLY RESTYLED) new 111" WB (THROUGH '79)

153 CID 4 (90 HP)
230 CID 6 (140 HP)
307 CID V8 (200 HP)

UP TO 295 HP AVAIL. 7.35 × 14 TIRES

SS OPTION $210. EXTRA

SALE PR.

all-new Nova at only $2261.00* (STD. CPE.)

1968 EASILY IDENTIFIED BY "CHEVY II" NAME ON TOP BORDER OF GRILLE.

SPORT WHEELS

OPTIONAL BUMPER GUARDS

RALLY WHEEL

53

Camaro

SS

Chevrolet

(SEE DATA AT LOWER LEFT)

68

new GRILLE

new "FLOW-THROUGH" VENTILATION ELIMINATES VENT PANES

new DASH

DUAL ROWS of SQUARE PORTS ATOP HOOD (SS MODELS)

SS

(STD. CAMARO H/T FROM $ 2917.)

230 CID 6 (140 HP) OR 327 CID V8 (210 HP) STD.

NOTE new FRONT and REAR SIDE (RECTANGULAR) SAFETY LIGHTS, AS REQUIRED BY LAW

7.35 × 14 TIRES

Chevrolet CORVAIR

$2457.

a true hardtop.
And it's Chevrolet's
lowest priced hardtop.

Corvair 500

"500" INTERIOR

Corvair Power Teams

ENGINES	TRANS-MISSIONS	AXLE RATIOS
95-HP TURBO-AIR 164 (Standard)	3-Speed (Standard)	3.55:1
	4-Speed (Extra-cost)	3.55:1
	Powerglide (Extra-cost)	3.27:1*
110-HP TURBO-AIR 164 (Extra-cost)	3-Speed (Standard)	3.27:1*
	4-Speed (Extra-cost)	3.27:1*
	Powerglide (Extra-cost)	3.55:1
140-HP TURBO-AIR 164 (Extra-cost)	3-Speed (Standard)	3.55:1
	4-Speed (Extra-cost)	3.55:1
	Powerglide (Extra-cost)	3.55:1

Positraction available for all ratios.
*3.55:1 may be specified.

1968 PRICES
SHOWN. $10
INCREASE, 1969.
SALES:
1968 = 12,977
1969 = 3,102

$2840.

MONZA CONVERTIBLE

new DASH

new SIDE SAFETY LTS.

(DISCONTINUED 5-14-69)

68-69

(FULL 1968-1969 LINE ILLUSTR.)

(NO 4-DR. HARDTOPS AFTER 1967)

OPT. LUGGAGE CARRIER

MONZA INTERIOR

OPT. WIRE WHEEL COVERS

MONZA SPT. CPE.

'68 Standard Safety Features

☐ Energy-absorbing steering column ☐ Seat belts with pushbutton buckles for *all* passenger positions ☐ Shoulder belts for driver and right front passenger with pushbutton buckles and convenient stowage provision on all models except convertibles ☐ Passenger-guard door locks with deflecting lock buttons — all doors ☐ Four-way hazard warning flasher ☐ Dual master cylinder brake system with warning light and corrosion-resistant brake lines ☐ Latches on front seat backs ☐ Dual-speed windshield wipers and washers ☐ Outside rearview mirror ☐ Back up lights. ☐ New side marker lights and parking lights that illuminate with headlights ☐ Padded instrument panel, sun visors, windshield pillars ☐ Reduced-glare instrument panel top, inside windshield mouldings, horn button, steering wheel hub, and windshield wiper arms and blades ☐ Inside day-night mirror with deflecting base ☐ Lane-change feature in direction signal control ☐ Safety armrests ☐ Thick-laminate windshield ☐ Soft, low-profile window control knobs, and coat hooks ☐ Energy-absorbing seat backs ☐ Yielding door and window control handles ☐ Energy-absorbing instrument panel with smooth contoured knobs and levers ☐ Tire safety rim ☐ Safety door latches and hinges ☐ Uniform shift quadrant ☐ Snag-resistant steering wheel hardware ☐ Fuel tank and filler pipe security.

$2721.

LARGER STD. 307 CID V8
(200 HP) USES REG. GAS
230 CID STD. 6
(140 HP)

MALIBU

CHEVELLE BY CHEVROLET

68

(RESTYLED)

AT CENTER:
Chevelle Nomad Custom
WAGON
(new)
$3303.
(3-ST.)

new WB
112" 2 DR.
116" 4 DR.
(THROUGH '77)

WITH
OPT.
VINYL TOP

SS-396

H/T = $3249.

STD.
230 CID 6
(140 HP)
307 CID V8
(200 HP)

FRONT VENT WINDOWS ELIMINATED

69

new
GRILLES

new
LOCKING STEERING COLUMN
and TRANS. LEVER

MALIBU H/T
$3025.
$3372 WITH
OPTIONAL ILLUS.

SS-396 PACKAGE

(also NOMAD,
GREENBRIER,
CONCOURS,
CONCOURS EST.
WAGONS AVAIL.)

56

CHEVROLET

ALL ENGINES
EXCEPT 427 CID V8s
USE REGULAR
GAS.

Impala

$3427.

new
PLASTIC
GRILLE

$3426.

(INTRO. 9-26-68)

ENGINES: 250 CID 6 (155 HP)
327 CID V8 (235 HP)
350 CID V8 (255 OR 300 HP)
396 CID V8
(265 HP)
427 CID V8
(335 OR 390 HP)

69
(RESTYLED)

new CONCEALED
HEADLIGHTS

Caprice

new
KINGSWOOD
ESTATE
(3-SEAT)
$4019.

wagon

new
BROOKWOOD,
TOWNSMAN, KINGSWOOD
and KINGSWOOD ESTATE
WAGONS

note FLARED
REAR FENDERS

(INTRO. 9-26-68)

CHEVY Nova

(NOVA REPLACES CHEVY II NAME)

new COWL LOUVRES

CHEVROLET EMBLEM NOW APPEARS ON TOP BORDER OF GRILLE.

69

153 CID 4 (90 HP)
230 CID 6 (140 HP)
307 CID V8 (200 HP)
SS OPTION : 350 CID V8 (300 HP)

"307" CID NUMBER ABOVE SIDE LIGHTS

V8 CPE. $2624.

PRICED FROM $2446. (4 - CYL. CPE.)

SS GRILLE

7.35 x 14 TIRES

REAR FENDER

Chevrolet **Camaro** (FINAL CONVERTIBLE AVAILABLE)

SS SPT. CPE. WITH RALLY SPORT EQUIP.

V-SHAPE and CRISS-CROSS PCS. IN new GRILLE→ (BLK.)

69

(CONTINUES TO FEB., 1970)

140 HP 6 TO 396 CID 325 HP V8 (EARLY 327 CID, 210 HP V8 REPL. BY new STD. 307 CID, 200 HP)

Step on the gas and it steps up performance.

SIDE LOUVRE DETAIL

new E78 × 14 TIRES

(AVAILABLE FOR EITHER SS OR Z-28)

Camaro's new Super Scoop

(IT OPENS ON ACCELERATION, PROVIDING COOL AIR TO CARBURETOR, ETC.)

SS has BIG V8 ENG., POWER DISC BRAKES, WIDE OVAL TIRES, and 3-SPEED FLOOR SHIFT.

'69 Corvette CHEVROLET a true American sports car.

note "STINGRAY" NAME ADDED, ON FRONT FENDERS

69

327 CID REPL. BY new 350 CID V8 (300 HP)

427 CID CONT'D. (390, 400, 430 OR 435 HP)

STINGRAY COUPE WITH ROOF SECTIONS REMOVED

(350 CID OR new 454 CID V8)

70-72

(300, 350, 370, 390 OR 460 HP '70)
('71 270, 330, 365, 425 HP OR 210, 275, 285, 325 SAE NET HP)
('72 200, 255 OR 270 HP)

new VENTS

('71)

new CRISS-CROSS PCS. IN GRILLE; SQUARE PK. LTS.

('71)

FROM $ 5126. ('70)
5548. ('71)
5532. ('72)
(CVT. PRICES)

(1972 CARRIES LIC. PLATE IN GRILLE CENTER, AS DO MANY PREV. MODELS.)

60

BROOKWOOD, TOWNSMAN, KINGSWOOD
KINGSWOOD ESTATE WAGONS
(FROM TOP, DOWN)
(119" WB)

70 Wagons MODELS) (7

new V-GRILLE

$3812.

(INTRO. 9-18-69)
3-ST. $4201.

2-ST. $4088.

KINGS. EST.

Impala

Right Car. Right Price. Right Now.

IMPALA CUSTOM H/T $3607.

2-DR. CUST. H/T

Caprice $3815.

(new MONTE CARLO IN SEPARATE SECTION.)

On the move: The Chevrolet '70s.

61

WAGONS FROM $3655.

CHEVELLE BY CHEVROLET WITH OPTIONAL Chevelle SS 396 PACKAGE

CHEVROLET On The Move.

TOP TO BOTTOM: NOMAD, GREENBRIER, CONCOURS, CONCOURS ESTATE WAGONS

new 2-TIER GRILLE

70

new 250 CID STD. 6 (155 HP)

UP TO 400 CID TURBO-JET V8 (330 HP)

MALIBU

H/T $3534.

MALIBU

SS PKG.

new TAIL-LIGHTS RECESSED IN REAR BUMPER

71

STD 250 CID 6 (145 HP)

STD 307 CID V8 (200 HP)

new GRILLE and BUMPERS. new CORNER LTS. new SINGLE HEADLTS.

H/T $3719.

1971. You've changed. We've changed.

CHEVROLET Monte Carlo

(2-DR. H/Ts ONLY)

70

(INTRO. 9-18-69)

$3123. (NEW)
$3464. (REG.)

116" WB

V-8 ENGINES :
350 CID (250 HP)
350 CID (300
400   265
400   330
454 CID (360 HP) (IN SS MODEL)

G78 × 15/B TIRES

IMITATION (VINYL)
CARPATHIAN BURLED ELM GRAIN
ON INSTRUMENT PANEL

71

new GRILLE

new RAISED ORNAMENT

$4041.

245, 270, 300 OR 365 HP

1971. You've changed.
We've changed.

CHEVY Nova 70

·SANDWICHES·FRIES·MALTS·

FROM $2554.
4-CYL. CPE.

1970 IS FINAL YR. FOR COWL LOUVRES.

new E78 x 14/B TIRES

new SQUARER SHAPE TO PARK./DIRECTIONAL LTS.

The Nova Coupe.

You didn't want it changed for the sake of change.

So we improved it for the sake of improvement.

$2637. ('71-6) 2613. ('72-6)
$2732. ('71-V8) 2703. ('72-V8)
Nova Sedan

CPES. FROM $2607.('71) 2585.('72)

250 CID 6
(145 HP)
(110 HP, '72)

307 CID V8
(200 HP)
(130 HP, '72)

RATED HP and PRICE CUTS, 1972

STD. CPE. W/O SIDE TRIM

71-72

1972 NOVAS ILLUSTRATED

DASH

65

(1971 – 1977) Chevrolet **VEGA**

PANEL EXPRESS

KAMMBACK WAGON

97" WHEELBASE

4 CYL.
OVERHEAD CAM
140 CID
90 HP
@ 4800 RPM

KNOWN AS
2300 SERIES
(BECAUSE ENG. IS IN 2300-cc CLASS)

new aluminum engine

HATCHBACK

71

(**NEW**)

FROM $2320.

2.53, 2.92 OR 3.36 GEAR RATIOS

STD. 2-DR.

(GTs ON NEXT PAGE)

NAMEPLATE READS:
"CHEVROLET VEGA 2300"
(ON 1971 and 1972 MODELS ONLY)

66

25 MPG.   **CHEVY'S NEW LITTLE VEGA.**

BROOKWD.

Impala

(BISCAYNE 4-DR. SED. FR. $3885.)

(INTRO. 9-29-70)
STD. HP
CUT (6-145)
(V8-245)

→ $4239.

new GRILLES

71

new 121½" WB

Caprice. ↗ CAPR. CUSTOM SED. 4-DR. H/T $4545.

Caprice
TYPE WITH MID-SIDE
TRIM SPEAR
(TYPE W/O, ABOVE RT.)

1971. You've changed. We've changed.

Impala $4257.

72

1972 SLOGAN: "CHEVROLET. BUILDING A BETTER WAY TO SEE THE U.S.A."

(FINAL BISCAYNE 4-DR. PRICED AT $3878.)

$4479.

FINE HORIZ PCS. IN IMPALA GRILLE ↗
350 CID V8 HP CUT AGAIN, (TO 165)

Caprice 4-Door Sedan.
(new)

WITH 400 CID V8 (170 HP) CAPRICE

FINAL 127" WB

SUBURBAN (CARRYALL) FR. $3640.

(INTRO. 9-23-71)

WAGON

WITH DISAPPEARING TAILGATE

CAPRICE GRILLE DETAIL

WHEEL COVER TYPE USED ON 2-DR. H/T

67

Chevrolet
Building a better way
to see the U.S.A.

Camaro Sport Coupe

Sport Coupe / Rally Sport / SS / Z28

DASH

STD. 307 C/D V8
(130 HP) (6
ALSO
AVAIL.)

72

FEWER PCS. IN *new*
STD. GRILLE

FROM
$3580.
(V8)

Rally Sport

Super Sport

"SS 350"

4- SPOKE
STEER. WHEEL

new
STD.
EQUIP.

"Z28"

Z28

note
"Z-28" ON
GRILLE

(REAR)

68

VEGA CHEVROLET

WAGON

GT.

2-DR. HATCH-BACK

(NEW)

BLACK GRILLE
A-70 × 13 TIRES
110 HP

(OTHER MODELS
CONTINUE FROM '71)

71 - 72

INTRODUCING THE VEGA GT.

We can show you only so much here. Available GT equipment includes special instrumentation: tach, amp and temp gauges, electric clock, and sport steering wheel.

GT DASH (ABOVE) has ROUND GAUGES

The Custom Interior

CUSTOM INTERIOR

Swing-out rear side window.

SWING-OUT REAR SIDE WINDOW (OPT.)

NO STYLING CHANGE, BUT SOME IMPROVEMENTS:
EASIER-SHIFTING 3 and 4-SPEED TRANSMISSIONS.
new WINDSHIELD WASHER CONTROL.
NAMEPLATE NOW READS "VEGA BY CHEVROLET."

Better belts and jack.

73

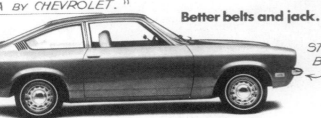

STRONGER BUMPERS

new ESTATE WAGON $2850.

Chevrolet introduces a neat little woody.

DASH

CHEVROLET MONTE CARLO

new GRILLE

72

$4009.

STD. 350 CID V8 CUT TO 165 HP

CUT TO 145 HP

new DASH

(RESTYLED)

73

new OPERA WINDOWS

3 CPE. MODELS AVAIL., FR. $3827.

STD., S, LANDAU MODELS

70

CHEVELLE

SCENE: 6 FLAGS AMUSEMT. PK., ATLANTA, GA.

250 CID 6 (110 HP)
307 CID V8 (130 HP)
350 CID V8 (165 OR 175 HP)
400 CID V8 (240 HP)
454 CID V8 (SS) (270 HP)

72

new GRILLE

Building a better way to see the U.S.A.

H/T ILLUSTR. WITH and W/O VINYL TOP

H/T $3683.

MALIBU

4-DR. SEDAN FROM $3486.

"HEAVY CHEVY" SPT. CPE. has BLACK GRILLE, SPECIAL STRIPING (INTRO. MID-'71)

DLX. CPE. $3599.

DLX. 4-DR. = $3566.

COLONNADE 4-DR.

Malibu $3711.

100 TO 245 HP (400 CID V8 DISCONTINUED '73 ONLY)

(CONT'D. NEXT PAGE)

73

new ENERGY-ABSORBING SAFETY BUMPERS

TOTALLY RESTYLED **DELUXE** COLONNADE CPE. and 4-DR. (ABOVE)

CHEVELLE

OPT. WHEEL COVERS

LAGUNA FRONT END IS ENTIRE BUMPER. OTHER new TYPE BUMPER AT TOP (GUARDS OPT.)

MALIBU →

MALIBU FR. $3997.

wagon

DLX. WAGON $3909. UP

CPE. $3743.

(MALIBU SS has "SS" IN CENTER OF BLACK GRILLE and on COWL.)

MALIBU

OPTION. SWING-OUT (90°) BUCKET SEATS

DASH (LAGUNA)

New Laguna

REAR

$4373.

CPE. $3932.

Laguna Estate

CHEVROLET

LOWEST-PRICED IS NOW THE **BELAIR**

73

4-DR. SEDAN AT $4018. → new GRILLES

$4196.

IMPALA

Impala

350 CID V8 CUT TO 145 HP
G78 × 15 TIRES
(L78 × 15, WAGONS)

New improved front bumper system that retracts on minor impact and hydraulically cushions the shock.

CAPRICE

DASH

IMPALA CUSTOM CPE. has INDENTED REAR WINDOW.

CAPRICE ESTATE WAGON FROM $4784.

OPTIONAL WIRE WHEEL COVERS

$4755.

$4496.

CAPRICE

AGAIN, CAPRICE has OWN GRILLE.

CAPRICE 400 CID V8 CUT TO 150 HP

1973 Chevrolet. Building a better way to see the U.S.A.

73

CHEVY Nova

(RESTYLED)

73

CPE. FR. $2589.

4-DR. FR. $2617.

250 CID 6 (100 HP)
307 CID V8 (115 HP)

Hatchback (New)

FROM $2738.

new 2-TONE ROOF ACCENT TRIM AVAILABLE (ON CAR ILLUSTR. ABOVE, CENTER)

4 TAIL-LIGHTS (new)

Chevrolet. Building a better way to see the U.S.A.

1973 DASH (BELOW)
(1974 DASH SIMILAR)

new GRILLE WITH PARK./DIRECTIONAL LIGHTS BUILT IN

NOVA/NOVA CUSTOM

Chevrolet **Camaro**

Z-28

307 CID V8 CUT TO 115 HP
(6 CYL. AVAIL.)

V8
SPORT
COUPE
$3608.

(NOT
AVAIL.
ON
Z-28)
TURBINE
I WHEEL

UNIROYAL
TIGER PAW F70-14

73

new
FRONT BUMPER

LT DASH
(LT = "LUXURY
TOURING")
$3884.
(V8)

↑
AVAIL.
ONLY
FOR
SPT.
CPE.
OR
RS

LT (new)
↓

RALLY
SPORT

($90. LESS
FOR 6-CYL.)

(SS
NOT
AVAIL.)

Chevrolet Corvette

Building a better way to see the U.S.A.

$5847.

$5621.

73

350 CID (190 HP @ 4400 RPM OR 250 HP @ 5200)

454 CID (275 HP @ 4400 RPM)

new GRILLE and PARKING LIGHTS
new RESILIENT BODY-COLORED BUILT-IN FRONT BUMPER

new DOMED HOOD

GR 70 x 15 TIRES

We gave it radials, a quieter ride, guard beams and a nose job.

CVT.

74

(350 OR 454 CID)

DASH

195,250 OR 270 HP

RESTYLED (sloping) REAR END

1974

76

CHEVROLET IMPALA

74

(BEL-AIR 4-DR. SED. PRICED AT $4473.)

IMPALA SPT. CPE. $4675.
CUSTOM CPE. $4742.

IMPALA SPT. SED. $4728.

DASH (CAPRICE)

new GRILLE TOTALLY ABOVE BUMPER. new FRONT CORNER LIGHTS ADDED.

CAPRICE MODELS FR. $4978. (4-DR.)

Caprice Estate wagon

FROM $5313.

New Flip-Down seats (wagon)

Caprice Classic

note GIANT new RR. QUARTER WINDOW ON **Caprice Classic**

CUST. CPE. $4996.

REAR

CVT. $5258.

Caprice

CHEVY Nova

74

250 CID 6 (100 HP)

new 350 CID V8 (145 HP)

DASH

CPE. FROM $3101.

CHEVROLET EMBLEM ADDED TO 1974 GRILLE

☐ **Nova Hatchback Hutch.** This handy camping tent attaches quickly and easily to Nova Hatchback models, transforming them into economy two-sleeper campers.

SEDAN FROM $3131.

new BRIGHT ANODIZED ALUMINUM HUBCAPS

☐ **Full wheel covers.** Shown left. ☐ Rally wheels with bright trim rings (included with SS). Shown right.

CUSTOM SS

SS has OWN GRILLE.

new "NOVA BY CHEVROLET" ON DECK (ALSO ON HOOD ON DRIVER'S SIDE)

HATCHBACK FROM $3225.

78

CHEVELLE BY CHEVROLET

(CHEVELLE DELUXE DISCONTINUED)

$2878* MALIBU 6 COUPE

$2873* MALIBU 6 SEDAN

(MALIBU, CLASSIC and CLASSIC EST. WAGONS AVAIL.)

Malibu Classic

Malibu Classic

LANDAU CPE.

$4590.

Malibu Classic: (NEW)

74

Engines	Power Rating*
Turbo-Thrift 250 Six	100-hp
Turbo-Fire 350 V8	145-hp
Turbo-Fire 350 V8	160-hp
Turbo-Fire 400 V8	150-hp
Turbo-Fire 400 V8	180-hp
Turbo-Jet 454 V8	235-hp

new GRILLES

(DURING 1974, MALIBU 6 CPE. PRICE INCREASED TO $3954.!)

new HOOD ORNAMENT (MAL.CLASSIC ONLY)

Malibu Classic Sedan

$4376.

Chevrolet makes sense for America.

S-3 GRILLE

LAGUNA TYPE S-3

$4504.

Chevelle Laguna Type S-3.

(note 2 AVAILABLE TOP STYLES)

NEW

S-3

(GR70 x 15 TIRES ON Laguna)

The Vega LX.
It's a deluxe version of the Notchback Coupe, with a vinyl roof cover.

(1975)

VEGA

DASH

GT DASH

VEGA GT.

new GRILLE

new TAIL-LIGHTS

FROM $2788. ('74)

Introducing the Cosworth Vega. ('75)

It's the special Vega with a number of hand-assembled, very expensive components.

The Cosworth engine comes out of Cosworth Engineering of England and makes use of sophisticated developments like twin camshafts and electronic fuel injection. It develops 120 horsepower at 5600 rpm and a torque of 115 lb.·ft. at 5200 rpm.

The Cosworth interior has special instrumentation.

The only exterior color available is the one shown here black, highlighted by gold decals, pinstriping and wheels.

Vega GT. To stripe or not to stripe?
That's up to you. GT sport stripes can be ordered in black or white.

CHROME "GT" (ON COWLS OF _UNSTRIPED_ GTs)

"COSWORTH TWIN CAM" DECAL ('75)

TWIN CAMS. $5979.

74-75

$3031. ('74)
$3314. ('75)

VEGA WAGONS

STD. WAGON

GT →

Vega Estate Wagon. $3259. ('74)

PANEL EXPRESS (NOT IN VEGA LINE AFTER 1975)

(Vega Estate GT. ALSO AVAIL.)

CHEVROLET Monte Carlo

Landau

TURBINE II WHEEL

DASH

S OR LANDAU TYPES (BOTH ILLUSTR.)

$4858.

new TAIL-LTS.

74

new GRILLE

$4614.

Monte Carlo S

SIMULATED WIRE WHEEL COVER →

new GR70 x 15/B TIRES

CHEVROLET MAKES SENSE FOR AMERICA

LANDAU CPE. $5273.

new TAIL-LTS.

75 new GRILLE

S COUPE $5003.

RALLY WHEEL

DASH

↑ new DLX. WHEEL COVER

Chevrolet **Camaro**

CHEVROLET MAKES SENSE FOR AMERICA.

STD. $4091. (LT=$4438.)

TOTALLY RESTYLED

74

Z-28

(6 CYL. $212. LESS)

250 CID (100 HP) 6-CYL. STILL AVAIL.; STANDARD V8 IS 350 CID, (WITH *new* 145 HP)

DASH

TAIL-LT. DETAIL

$4424. Sport Coupe or Type LT. ($4796.)
(105 HP 6 CYL. $145 LESS)
SPORT COUPE

2-TONE

WITH RALLY SPORT TRIM

('75)

75 -76

new RECTANGULAR EMBLEM, NOW ON HOOD *and* REAR DECK

camaro

('75) **TYPE LT** LT WOODGRAINED

NOVA SIX.

$3218.

* REG. $3966.

(RESTYLED)

'75

EPA mileage:
16 city,
21 highway.

HATCHBACK
CPE. $4214.

NOVA

FR 78 x 14
TIRES
(EXCEPT ON
$3966. "S"
CPE. AT TOP,
LEFT)

NOVA CUSTOM

$4270.

So we've distinguished the exterior of our '75 Nova LN—front, rear and sides—with this classic LN emblem.

It appears inside, too (on the steering wheel), along with some of the nicest things that ever happened to a compact.

250 CID 6 (105 HP)
new 262 CID V8
(110 HP)

$4650.

LN (new)

DASH (LN)

LN 4-DR.
$4663.

CHEVROLET MAKES SENSE FOR AMERICA

83

CHEVELLE
coupe.
$3407.*

MALIBU
The lowest-priced sedan.
$3402.*

Malibu Wagon

22% higher gas mileage with standard V8

1975

$4989.

MALIBU CLASSIC

CPE.

Malibu Classic instrument panel, with new speedometer calibrated in both miles per hour (mph) and kilometers per hour (kph).

$5412. WAGON (MAL. CLASSIC ESTATE) → (3-ST.)

(ALSO AVAIL. W/O GRAIN)

SEDAN
$4744.

250 CID 6 (105 HP)
350 CID V8 (145 OR 155 HP)
400 CID V8 (175 HP)
454 CID V8 (215 HP)

22M-72

NEW, 75

catalytic converter.

(RESTYLED FRONT and REAR ENDS)

new SLOPING FRONT ON

LAGUNA TYPE S-3

$4867.

LAGUNA TYPE S-3

DASH

(ALSO AVAIL. INTO 1976.)

(SINCE 1975)

Chevrolet
Chevrolet makes sense for America

Monza

Monza 2+2

97" WB   87 HP
4-CYL. (140 C/D)
OR
2 V-8s)

THE NEW MONZA "S"
HATCHBACK COUPE.
$3946.

75-76

COWL LETTERING

18½-GAL. FUEL TANK

POWER VENT SLOTS

TROMPE L'OEIL WHEEL COVERS. That's French for "fool the eye." Which is what these standard wheel covers do beautifully. They look like expensive metal wheels but they're tough molded polycast.

$4250.

2+2

BR 78 × 13 TIRES

"V8 4.3 LITRE" PLAQUE DESIGNATES A 262½ CID V8 (110 HP) (125 HP, 305 CID V8 AVAIL. ALSO)

85

CHEVROLET

FINAL BEL-AIR

BEL AIR 4-DOOR SEDAN

IMPALA

(FINAL CVT.)

IMPALA 4-DOOR

NEW CATALYTIC CONVERTER
(Standard, all '75 Chevrolet cars, and trucks 6,000 GVW and below.)

75

LANDAU CPE. WITH LARGE QUARTER WINDOWS STILL AVAILABLE

CAPRICE CLASSIC SPORT SEDAN

Caprice Classic

(new)

CATALYTIC CONVERTER (SINCE 1975)

Chevy Suburban

$4707. UP 129" WB

CHEVROLET MAKES SENSE FOR AMERICA

FROM $5758.

Now that makes sense

CAPRICE ESTATE

IMPALA TAIL-LTS.

4190-ED

$5068.

EPA M.P.G. 13 CITY, 18 HWY. (w. STD. 350-2 V8)

IMPALA 76

$5323.

← NO MID-SIDE CHROME STRIP.

Impala **S**

SEDAN

(CONT'D. NEXT PAGE)

INTERIOR

86

CHEVROLET 76
(CONT'D.)

$5638.

(FINAL 4-DR. H/T)

$5603.

Caprice Classic

note DIFFERENCES IN WHEEL COVERS

1976. Chevrolet makes room for America.

(TOTALLY RESTYLED)

Now that's more like it.

Impala

IMPALA RR.

The 1977 Caprice Classic Sedan

New SIZE

$5967. 116" WB

CAPRICE CLASSIC CPE. $5917.

77

Caprice Classic.

22 mpg. hwy.	17 mpg. city

REAR

CID 6 (110 HP) STD. 305 CID V8 (145 HP)

DASH (CAPRICE)

20.2-cubic-foot trunk

SUBURBAN $5087. UP

FROM $6427. CAPR. ESTATE

WAGON

Chevrolet

Corvette

75-76

(350 CID ONLY FROM 165 HP ('75) 180 HP ('76))

INTRODUCING A MORE EFFICIENT CORVETTE.

new HIGH ENERGY IGNITION

new CATALYTIC CONVERTER

(1975 IS FINAL CONVERT.)

The roll of radials. Corvette's Efficiency System extends right to the road and those special GR70-15 steel-belted radial ply tires.

IMPROVED BUMPER SYSTEM ('75)

DASH

The only one.

$ 9504.

new EMBLEM

77

new BLACK WINDSHIELD POSTS

FRONT SIDE LIGHT LENS

• Soft-Ray tinted glass.
• Black windshield posts give new "thin pillar" look.

180 OR 210 HP

89

HATCHBACK $4366.

$3283*
Nova 4-Door Sedan
(REG. $4232.)

Nova

E78 × 14/B TIRES ON STD. NOVA

Nova SS Coupe.

250 CID 6 (105 HP)
305 CID V8 (140 HP)

76 (Introducing Concours.)

note THAT GRILLE OF NEW CONCOURS has HEAVY PANEL OF BRIGHTWORK ABOVE

Concours Coupe

Concours

4-Door Sedan
$4780.

(new)

$4745.

CONCOURS has HOOD ORNAMENT and FULL-LENGTH SIDE TRIM.
(CONCOURS TIRE SIZE = FR 78 × 14/B)
CONCOURS HATCHBACK AVAIL., AT $4922.

NOVA DASH RESEMBLES ILLUSTRATED CONCOURS DASH, BUT DOES NOT have WOOD GRAIN.

• Instrument cluster with rosewood vinyl accents, smoked lenses, bright framing.
• Available electric clock.
• Built-in heater and defroster system.
• Concours identification on steering wheel.
• Available Four-Season air conditioning and AM/FM stereo radio.
• Cigarette lighter.
• Glove compartment light and lock.
• Soft-rim steering wheel with cushioned center.
• Color-keyed steering wheel with wood-grain vinyl accent.

Concours

'76 Chevelle.
A size whose time has come.

REG. $4711.

$5185. (LANDAU)

MALIBU CLASSIC

76

new GRILLES
(MAL. CLASSIC *has* OWN 4 HEADLIGHTS, MESH-TYPE GRILLE) →

Two roomy Chevelles priced under $3671. (SALE)
26 MPG Highway, 18 MPG City, EPA.*

MALIBU

← REG. $4746.

* = WITH 250 CID 6 (105 HP) 20 HWY., 14 CITY
WITH 305 CID V8 (new, 140 HP)
(454 CID V8 DISCONT'D.)

Smart, complete, mid-size Chevelle.

(NO MORE TYPE 9-3)

MALIBU WAGON

$5466.

SALE: $3885.

MALIBU

MALIBU CLASSIC

$5651.

new GRILLES, FEWER ENG. CHOICES

77

250 CID 6 (110 HP)
305 CID V8 (145 HP)
350 CID V8 (170 HP)

DASH (MALIBU CLASSIC)

$5327.

(illustr. LARGE SIDE MIRROR IS OPTIONAL.)

TAIL-LT. DETAILS

91

Monte Carlo

When a car makes you feel good about its looks, that's style. When it makes you feel good about yourself, that's character.

76

DASH

new GRILLE

w/o VINYL TOP $5218.

DELUXE WH. COVER

WITH VINYL TOP → $5511.

Wire wheel covers.

Rally wheels.

Turbine II wheels. (Std. on Landau.)

new TAIL-LIGHTS

new 305 CID V8 (140 HP)

LANDAU CPE.

305 CID (145 HP) V8, OR 350 CID (170 HP) V8

Like you, it's an original.

w/o VINYL TOP

$5539.

new TAIL-LIGHTS

LANDAU CPE. W/VINYL TOP

RALLY WHEELS

1977 DASH IS SIMILAR IN MOST RESPECTS TO 1976 TYPE ILLUSTR.

$5869.

DELUXE WHEEL CVR.

77

GR 70 × 15 TIRES

new SPORT WHEEL COVER

new GRILLE

VEGA CHEVROLET

- Soft-rim steering wheel with cushioned center.
- 80 mph in white numbers with metric equivalents in blue.
- Available AM/FM radio and accessory electric clock.

1976 SLOGAN: "built to take it."

OPTIONAL SUN-ROOF

- Inside hood release.

DASH

- Function symbols in headlights, cigarette lighter and radio control knobs.

SPORT CPE.

new LARGER TAIL-LTS.

new GRILLE

HATCHBACK

wagon
$3540. ('76)
$3836. ('77)

The 1976 Vega Dura-Built 140 engine is so good it's backed up by a 5-year or 60,000-mile guarantee.

ALSO AVAIL.: GT WAGON, GRAINED ESTATE, ESTATE GT WAGONS

1977 GT

76-77

(FINAL '76 COSWORTH PRICED AT $6135.)

"Today's Vega"

(1977 SLOGAN)

33 mpg highway/24 mpg city (EPA).

- Tachometer, temperature gauge and voltmeter.
- Wood-grain vinyl accents.
- Electric clock.
- 80 mph in white numbers with metric equivalents in blue.
- Assist handle built into instrument panel pad.

- Inside hood release.
- Four-spoke sport steering wheel.
- Available Four-Season air conditioning and AM/FM radio.
- Cigarette lighter.

GT DASH

93

Chevette
Chevrolet's new kind of American car.

(SINCE 1976)
(SOLD BY 6,030 CHEVROLET DEALERS)

85 CID 4 (52 HP)
(97.6 CID. 60 HP AVAIL.)

EPA rating
- **40 MPG highway**
- **28 MPG city**

94.3" WB

76

13-GAL. FUEL TANK
155×80-13 TIRES

RALLY SPORT OR WOODY TRIM AVAIL.

$3314. SCOOTER has NO BACK SEAT

INTERNATIONAL TAILLIGHTS. It's the red, white, and amber combination found in most world-type cars. Outside—stop. Middle—signal. Inside—backup.

3.7 OR 4.11 G.R.

43 MPG
EPA HIGHWAY

31 MPG
EPA CITY ESTIMATE

Shown below is Sandpiper's special interior trim.

Bright and happy. That's Sandpiper with the special Custom Interior that features richly patterned "Reef" cloth-and-vinyl upholstery in tones of Yellow, Cream and Gold. Carpeting, instrument panel and seat belts are Yellow Gold. Also included: deluxe door trim, woodgrain vinyl accents, sport steering wheel, day-night rearview mirror, carpeted cargo area and added acoustical insulation.

Sandpiper

BUMPER RUB STRIPS AND GUARDS. Front and rear. Protect from minor dings. Add styling appeal.

JZX 187

(OPT.)

RALLY SPORT Pkg.

It'll drive you happy.

new SANDPIPER PKG. OPT.

ZIX 362

2-DR. $3540.

77

new 57 HP (85 CID ENG.) OPT. SIDE TRIM STRIP AVAIL.

(OPT.)

SWING-OUT WINDOWS.

SPECIAL INSTRUMENTATION. For the well-informed driver. Has tachometer and voltmeter. Included with available Rally Sport equipment.

94

CHEVY NOVA

EXTRA-LG. BUMPER GUARDS ONLY ON POLICE CARS.

SEDAN $4539.

CPE. FR. $4489.

77 new GRILLES

UNIQUE MESH GRILLE ON

NOVA RALLY

(BECOMES THE NOVA CUSTOM RALLY IN '78, WITH SIMILAR STYLING)

new 110 HP (6) 145 HP (V8)

THE FINAL **CONCOURS**

TRIPLE TAIL LTS. (new)

$5073.

CONCOURS GRILLE

Concours: A world class luxury compact from Chevrolet.

SEE WHAT'S NEW TODAY IN A CHEVROLET.

26 MPG. HWY., 19 CITY

CHEVY NOVA 4-DR. $3823.*

*(REG. $4852.)

2-DR. $3702.*

*(REG. $4777.)

EMBLEM ADDED ABOVE GRILLE, new BUMPERS (STD. NOVA)

78

HOOD ORNAMENT NOT INCL. ON new CUSTOM

NOVA CUSTOM (FORMERLY THE CONCOURS)

95

Chevrolet
Camaro

Z28

Z-28 SPOILER

$5767.

SPECIAL PAINT JOB ON Z-28

STD. 305 CID V8 (145 HP) OR 250 CID 6 (100 HP)

SPT. CPE. $5082.

STD. E/FR78 x 14/B TIRES

(Z-28 = GR70 x 15)

Z28 77

RETURNS!

Z-28 350 CID V8 has 170 HP (ENG. AVAIL. FOR "LT" also)

SEE WHAT'S NEW TODAY IN A CHEVROLET.

OVERHEAD VIEW of new T-BAR ROOF AVAIL.

new ALL-MOLDED FRONT APPEARS "BUMPERLESS"

(6-CYL. has new 110 HP)

78

Camaro Z28 has new SLANTING LOUVRES on SIDE of COWL.

$6236.

new T-BAR AVAIL.

(STD. $5562. UP)

DASH

LT FR. $5962.

SEE WHAT'S NEW TODAY IN A CHEVROLET.

Silver Anniversary Corvette.

new FASTBACK REAR WINDOW **78**

new

25TH ANNIVERSARY EMBLEM

P225/60R×15 TIRES

$10,286.

CHEVROLET

$ 6042.

(INTRO. THURS., 10-8-77)

SEE WHAT'S NEW TODAY IN A CHEVROLET.

EPA M.P.G. 17 CITY, 24 HWY. WITH 250 CID 6 (110 HP)

305 CID V8 (145 HP)

POWER SKY ROOF AVAIL. (above)

IMPALA

78

new GRILLES

CAPRICE CLASSIC

WAGON

$ 6460.

Impala

CAPR. CLSSC. (REAR) ('79)

new HORIZ. STRIPS ACROSS CORNER LTS.

Impala

new GRILLES

79

Caprice Classic

$ 7324. America has driven it to the top.

$ 6829. UP

305 CID V8 CUT TO 130 HP

350 CID V8 (170 HP)

$ 7754. UP

new 108" WB

CHEVROLET

Monte Carlo

78

RESTYLED

LANDAU CPE. $6451.

SPORT CPE. $6086.

new 205/70R×14 TIRES

DASH

105 HP, 231 CID V-6 IS new STANDARD ENGINE. 305 CID V8 ALSO AVAIL. (145 HP)

The Third Generation Monte Carlo.
A new dimension in affordable luxury.

DASH SIMILAR TO 1978

200/231 CID V6s (94/115 HP)
267/305 CID V8s STD. (125/160 HP) (350 CID V8 AVAIL.)

T-TOP (OPT.)

79

new FRONT and REAR CORNER LIGHT LENSES (w. HORIZONTAL STRIPS)

RALLY WHEEL

SPORT CPE. $6711. (LANDAU CPE. $7561.)

Chevette

STANDARD: Deluxe grille.

STANDARD: AM radio. | STANDARD: Console. | STANDARD: Swing-out rear windows. | STANDARD: Wheel trim rings. | STANDARD: Cigarette lighter. | STANDARD: Color-keyed instrument panel. | STANDARD: Glove compartment lock.

'78

new 4-DR. $3805. (97.3" WB)

MANY *new* STANDARD FEATURES (ILLUSTR.)

STANDARD: Carpeting.

2-Door

$3695.

'78 Chevette. A lot more car for a lot less money.*

97.6 CID 4 (63 HP) NOW STANDARD

STANDARD: Bumper rub strips. | STANDARD: Sport steering wheel. | STANDARD: Body side moldings.

STANDARD: Fully synchronized 4-Speed transmission.

SCOOTER $3340. WITH FEWER FEATURES

BEST-SELLING SMALL CAR IN AMERICA.

70 HP

79

new GRILLE

SCOOTER (NO SIDE TRIM) $3724.

('79)

$4220.

$4100.

1979 and 1980 DASH SIMILAR EXCEPT FOR MINOR CHANGES IN SPEC. INSTRUMENTATION PKG. (illustrated)

74 HP AVAIL.

2-TONE PAINT AVAIL.

70 HP

('80)

80

new 4-PIECE WRAP-AROUND TAIL-LIGHTS

CHEVROLET 100377

A lot of car for the money.
1980

$4756. (2-DR. and SCOOTER AVAIL.)

TACHOMETER. Constantly monitors engine speed.

Chevrolet MONZA

4 CYL. or V6

(V8 AVAIL. ALSO)

WAGON ('78)

WAGON (1979 FINAL YR., AT $4646.)

NEW ('78)

SALE **$3698**

(ESTATE WAG. ALSO, '78 ONLY)

EPA ESTIMATES **34/24** HWY CITY

WAGON **78-80**

new GRILLES

BODY SIDE MOULDINGS BECOME STD. EQUIPMENT IN 1979.

COUPE

$4080. ('78)
4517. ('79)
5041. ('80)
(4497. SALE)

Monza 2+2

DASH

('80)

(1979 MODELS ILLUSTRATED, UNLESS OTHERWISE INDICATED.)

2+2 Sport

WITH OPT. "SPYDER" PACKAGE

CHEVELLE

NOW KNOWN AS

CHEVY MALIBU

MALIBU CLASSIC **WAGON**

MPG
29 HWY.
21 EPA
WITH
200 CID V6

$6025.

EST. $6221.

23 HWY., 16 EPA
231 CID V6

$5543.

95 TO 170 HP

NEW-SIZE

78

new SHORTER 108" WB

(RESTYLED)

DASH (MALIBU CLASSIC)

MALIBU, **MALIBU CLASSIC**

Now SHARE GRILLE, BUT MAL. CLASSIC has CHROME TRIM AROUND WINDOWS, ETC. →

new 200, 231 CID V6s
(305, 350 CID V8s ALSO)

(SPEC. INSTRUMENTATION PKG. has SMALL ROUND GAUGES.)

" SEE WHAT'S NEW TODAY IN A CHEVROLET. "

1978

↑ 5902.

22 EPA estimated MPG / **28** Highway estimate

"A FRESH NEW SLICE OF APPLE PIE"

$6512.

MALIBU CLASSIC

(DASH LIKE '78, BUT WITH "Malibu Classic" LETTERING AT RT.)
(new 267 CID V8 ADDED)

79
new GRILLE

MALIBU 4-D SEDAN

$4915. (SALE)

VALUE IS WHAT MAKES A MALIBU A CHEVROLET.

MAL. PRICED FROM $6543.

MPG: 20 EPA 26 HWY.

new GRILLE

80
Malibu CLASSIC

$7063.
↓

102

Nova

HATCHBACK $5260.

NOVA

Nova Models.

RALLY WHEELS

RALLY → (note RALLY INSIGNIA and BODY STRIPES

79

250 CID 6 (115 HP)
305 CID V8 (130 HP) OR 350 CID V8 (170 HP)

new GRILLE WITH ALL-HORIZONTAL PCS.

BUMPER RUB STRIP and GUARDS OPTION.

DASH (NOVA CUSTOM)

Nova Custom Models. $5406.

FINAL NOVA. REPLACED BY CHEVY CITATION FOR 1980.

WIRE WHEEL COVER

CABRIOLET ROOF COVER (OPT.)

$5306.

GRILLE TOP BORDER BEARS "Chevrolet" NAME.

POL

103

STD. 250 CID 6 (115 HP) OR 305 CID V8 (130 HP)

Camaro Sport Coupe $6252.

Camaro Rally Sport

79

(FULL LINE ILLUSTR.)

RS FROM $6661.

WITH T-TOP (OPTIONAL)

Z-28 DASH ILLUSTR. AT TOP OF PAGE

"Z-28" SIDE DECAL NOW ON DOOR

Z-28 GRILLE

new Camaro Berlinetta

Berlinetta

Z-28 has 350 C/D V8 (170 HP)

1979 Camaro Z28 $7167.

$6995.

CAMARO. THE HUGGER.

Chevrolet CORVETTE

79

DASH AND CONS.

FIBERGLASS BODIES ON ALL CORVETTES (1953 ON)

P225/70R ×15 OR P255/60R ×15 TIRES

new REAR SPOILER

$11,536.

350 CID V8 STD. (195-225 HP)

(GDYR. GT TIRES, 1980)

$13,104.

new 2-PC. CORNERING LTS.

(RESTYLED)

80

(new 305 CID V8 ALSO AVAIL.) 180-190 HP

new FRONT END WITH AIR DAM; LOW-PROFILE HOOD

CHEVROLET

EST RANGE*

450 CITY **650** HWY

WITH 25-GAL. FUEL TANK

18 26
EPA EST. MPG*   HWY. ESTIMATE
WITH STD. 229 V6 ENG. (115 HP)

IMPALA WAGON FR. $7526.

IMPALA

IMPALA SPT. CPE.

$7105.

IMPALA SEDAN $7214.

new P205/75R×15 TIRES (P225 ON WAGONS)

80

CAPRICE CLASSIC LANDAU CPE. has BRIGHTWORK BAR EXTENDING UP OVER ROOF $7954.

STD. 267 CID V8 (120 HP) 305 OR 350 CID AVAIL.

DASH (CAPRICE CLASSIC)

RICH WOODGRAIN EFFECTS

CAPRICE CLASSIC

SEDAN $7635.

CAPR. $8125. UP ESTATE WAGON

BOTH IMPALA AND CAPRICE CLASSIC GRILLES ARE **NEW**

New engines.

106

CHEVROLET MONTE CARLO

80

WITH T-TOP AND 2-TONE PAINT OPTION ↙

new GRILLE has FEWER PIECES. 4 new RECTANGULAR HEADLIGHTS →

SPORT CPE. $7040.

LOW SIDE LIGHT REPLACES CORNER TYPE. ↖

new DASH

LANDAU CPE. $7288.

new STYLE OF RALLY WHEEL ↓

P-205/70R-14 TIRES STANDARD

115 HP, 229 CID V-6 IS new STD. ENG. (231 CID IN CALIFORNIA) (110 HP)

(TURBO V6 AVAIL.)

267/305 CID V8s AVAIL. (120/155 HP)

Camaro
Chevrolet

SPORT COUPE. $6699.

AVAILABLE OPTION

80

TAIL-LT. DETAILS

BERLINETTA

$7462.

new STD. ENGINES
229 CID 6 (115 HP)
267 CID V8 (120 HP)
(305 CID V8 AVAIL.)

RALLY SPORT FROM $7116.

AVAIL. FOR RALLY SPT. OR SPT. CPE.

NOT TO BE CONFUSED WITH WIRE WHEELS SHOWN ON BERLINETTA

Z28 DASH

11

EPA MPG:
20 CITY
26 HWY.
(6)

Z 28 FOR 1980. THE MAXIMUM CAMARO.
with 350 CID V8 (new 190 HP) 129

(STARTS WITH 1980 MODEL) **CHEVROLET** Citation (FRONT WHEEL DRIVE)
A whole new kind of compact car.

STD. DASH

Club Coupe. → $6300.

Custom Interior DASH (ROUND GAUGES) (NEW) **80**

SLIP STREAM STYLING

Full Wheel Covers.

TRANSVERSE ENGINE
104.9" WB
P185/80R x 13 TIRES

2-DR. HATCHBACK $6427. (STD. CPE = $5965.)

(ALSO KNOWN AS "CHEVY" CITATION.)

4-DR. HATCHBACK $6293.

(INTRO. 4-19-79)

EPA MPG 24 CITY, 38 HWY. WITH 151 CID 4 (90 HP)

173 CID V6 (110 OR 115 HP) ALSO AVAIL.

SPORT PACKAGE - $500.

X-11 WITH SPECIAL PAINT JOB, P205/70R-13 TIRES

X-11 STEERING WHEEL

(X-11 CL. CPE. ALSO AVAIL.)

"THE FIRST CHEVY OF THE '80s"

109

CHEVROLET

(TRUCKS SINCE 1918)
BY CHEVROLET DIVISION OF
GENERAL MOTORS CORP.,
DETROIT.

"T" has 13-GALLON FUEL TANK UNDER SEAT, and 25-M.P.H. SPEED GOVERNOR.

('18)

490	1/2 TON			
G	3/4		120" WB	5.42 GR
T	1		125	

18-22
4 CYLS. (THROUGH '28)

SERIES T
1 TON CAP. 125" W.B.

33 × 4 TIRES ('20-'22) "T" FRONT TIRE SIZE ONLY

31 × 4

ZENITH CARB., REMY IGNITION

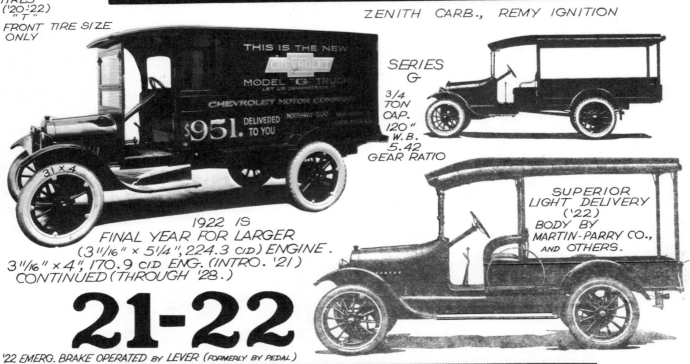

THIS IS THE NEW
CHEVROLET
MODEL "G" TRUCK
LET US DEMONSTRATE
CHEVROLET MOTOR COMPANY
NORTHWAY 600
$951. DELIVERED TO YOU

31 × 4

SERIES G
3/4 TON CAP. 120" W.B. 5.42 GEAR RATIO

SUPERIOR LIGHT DELIVERY ('22) BODY BY MARTIN-PARRY CO., AND OTHERS.

1922 IS FINAL YEAR FOR LARGER (3"/16" × 5 1/4", 224.3 CID) ENGINE.
3"/16" × 4", 170.9 CID ENG. (INTRO. '21) CONTINUED (THROUGH '28.)

21-22

'22 EMERG. BRAKE OPERATED BY LEVER (FORMERLY BY PEDAL)

(NO MORE 3/4-TON TRUCKS UNTIL 1937, BUT 1/2-TON MODELS CONTINUE.)

UTILITY EXPRESS CHASSIS

SERIES D

1-TON

31 × 4

('23)

"D"   "H"

23-24

120" WB (THROUGH EARLY '25)

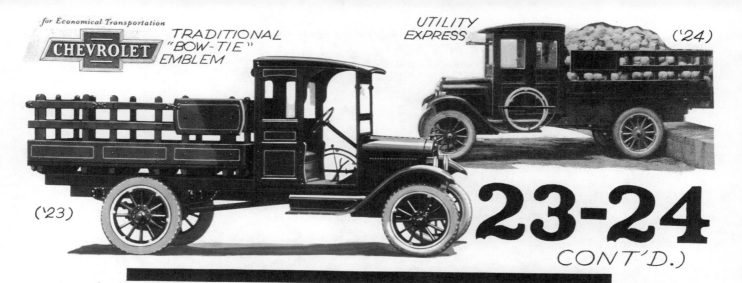

for Economical Transportation

CHEVROLET

TRADITIONAL "BOW-TIE" EMBLEM

UTILITY EXPRESS

('24)

('23)

23-24
CONT'D.)

"SUPERIOR" NAME CONT'D. FROM '24.

103" WB ON ½ TON CHASSIS
124" " " 1-TON REPLACES
120" ('26.)

EARLY '25 IS MODEL "M."

25-26

LATE '25 "R" WITH HERCULES BODY

STAKE

LATE '26 MODEL "X" has NEW CHEVROLET-BUILT, FULLY ENCLOSED BODY.

"LM" HAS 1 TON CAP., 124" W.B., 30×5 TIRES ALL AROUND, AS DOES 1926 MODEL "X."

DELUXE 1-TON PANEL

('27)

OPEN EXPRESS

27
"CAPITOL"

DASH

new RADIATOR HAS DIP AT CENTER OF UPPER PAN.

CHEVROLET

ROOF-VISOR (LT. MODEL)

UTILITY TRUCK *with* 4-SPEED TRANSMISSION *and* 4-WH. BRAKES (8-28)

1927-1928 TRUCKS DO NOT HAVE STEERING COLUMN LOCK (AS USED ON '27-'28 CHEVROLET CARS.)

IN 1-TON, 124"-W.B. MODELS, EARLY '28 IS "LO," LATER '28 IS "LP."

28

JENESEN FANCY GROCERIES

TELEPHONE MAIN 0-100

4-WHEEL BRAKES ON LT. DUTY MODELS

Illustrating the Light Delivery Chassis equipped with Panel Body

29 × 4.40 TIRES (30 × 5 REAR ON 1-TON)

CHEVROLET

SEDAN DELIVERY STYLING MORE LIKE THAT OF A CHEVROLET CAR.

('29)

NEW 6-CYL. ENGINE IN 1929

"INTERNATIONAL" "UNIVERSAL"

29-30

The Utility 1½ Ton Chassis with Chevrolet cab, equipped with power dump body built of reinforced steel to withstand concentrated weight. Popular among coal dealers, contractors, road builders, etc.

STARTING 1930, SOME CANADIAN MODELS BEAR THE "MAPLE LEAF" NAME.

194 CID (THROUGH '32)
'29 : AC (½ TON) 107" WB (THROUGH '30)
LQ (1½ TON) 131" WB

ALL MODELS HAVE 4-WH. BRAKES IN 1930.

1930 MODEL HAS new DASH with SMALL CIRCULAR GAUGES (INCLUDING ELECTRIC FUEL GA.) ILLUSTRATED AT RIGHT →

1½ Ton

POWER DUMP COMBINATION ('30)

The 1½ TON CHASSIS

50 HP and 4-SPEED TRANSMISSION

FINAL YEAR FOR THIS STYLE of LIGHT DISC WHEELS.

STAKE ('30)

↰ SPARE TIRE and RIM MOUNTED HORIZONTALLY

'30 : AD (½ TON)
LR (1½ TON) (LATER BECOMES "LS") 131" WB

DELIVERY MODELS OF 1930

SEDAN DELIVERY

1½-TON CANOPY EXPRESS

PANEL DELIVERY

LIGHT DELIVERY

CHEVROLET

31

"INDEPENDENCE"

IND. COM.	½ TON	109" WB
Y UTILITY	1½	131
UL DUAL	1½	157

(ALSO KNOWN AS AE (½ T.)
LT, MA, MB, MC, MD
(1½ T.) MODELS)

50 HP @
2600 RPM.
CARTER CARB.

4.75 × 19 TIRES
ON ½-TON.
(ALSO EARLY '32)

new LONGER GROUP
OF MORE
HOOD LOUVRES,
SET IN SURROUNDING
PANEL.

SEDAN DELIVERY
(EARLY MODEL *with* TWO-BLADE
BUMPERS)

LATER MODEL *with*
SINGLE BLADE BUMPER

DISC WHEELS
STILL AVAILABLE,
BUT WIRE WHEELS
TYPICAL AFTER 1930.

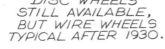

Open Cab Pick-up—Pick-up box 66 inches long, 45 inches wide and 13 inches deep. Body sides are so designed that they meet floor at right angles, permitting compact loading and generous capacity. Roadster-type cab. Disc wheels. Price of complete unit $440.

1½-TON
OPEN EXPRESS
(HEAVY PICKUP)
with 157" WB,
30 × 5
TIRES

31

"INDEPENDENCE" (CONT'D.)

PICKUP (CLOSED CAB) (66" BOX)

CHEVROLET

NEW VIBRATOR HORN BELOW LEFT HEADLIGHT

STAKE

new 157" WB MODEL (NOTE EXTRA SET OF STAKES)

Light Delivery Panel Truck—Body loading space 72 inches long, 45 inches wide, 48 inches high. Side panels heavily insulated for silence and load protection. Comfortable coupe-type driver's compartment. Disc wheels standard. Price of complete unit $555.

1½-Ton 131-inch Stake Truck—Body 108 inches long and 82 inches wide, with 42-inch stakes. Hardwood sills and uprights, heavily ironed. Inset stake pockets in steel rub rail. Hinged side section. Price of complete unit $710. Dual wheels optional, $25 extra.

1½-Ton Panel Truck—Body loading space is 108 inches long, 60 inches wide and 52 inches high. Side panels heavily insulated, as in light delivery panel truck. Comfortable coupe-type driver's compartment. Disc wheels standard. Price of complete unit $760.

1½-Ton 131-inch Canopy Express Truck—Body loading space 108 inches long, 45 inches wide and 52 inches high. Sheet steel and hardwood construction. Waterproof curtains, sides and rear, standard. Side screens extra. Disc wheels. Price of complete unit $750.

Light Delivery Canopy Express—Body loading space 72 inches long, 45 inches wide and 48 inches high. Waterproof curtains, sides and rear, standard equipment. Screen extra. Sedan-type roof. Coupe-type cab. Disc wheels. Price of complete unit $550.

1½-Ton 131-inch High and Wide Express Truck—Body 108 inches long and 60 inches wide. Paneled sides. Body mounted on 6 heavy cross sills. Comfortable coupe-type cab. Price of complete unit $715. Dual wheels optional, $25 extra.

1½-Ton 157-inch High and Wide Express Truck—For loads requiring extra large floor space. Body 144 inches long, 60 inches wide. Paneled sides. Flare boards securely braced. Body mounted on 6 heavy sills. Dual wheels standard. Price of complete unit $800.

1½-Ton 131-inch Cab and Platform Truck—Loading space 108 inches long, 82 inches wide. Floor 1½ inches thick. Floor made of hardwood, with steel angle rub rails. Six heavy hardwood cross sills. Price of complete unit $680. Dual wheels optional, $25 extra.

1½-Ton 157-inch Cab and Platform Truck—For those who require extra large loading space. Platform 12 feet long, 82 inches wide. Floor 1½ inches thick. Platform mounted on seven hardwood cross sills. Dual wheels standard. Price of complete unit $770.

1½-Ton 131-inch Stock Rack Truck—Floor space 108 inches long, 82 inches wide. Rack 60 inches high. Hardwood uprights, steel rub rail and floor supported on six heavy cross sills. Chevrolet cab. Price of complete unit $730. Dual wheels optional, $25 extra.

1½-Ton 157-inch Stock Rack Truck—Designed for loads that require extra floor space. Body 144 inches long, 82 inches wide. Rack 60 inches high. Floor supported on six heavy cross sills. Dual wheels standard equipment. Price of complete unit $830.

115

new SYNCHRO-MESH TRANS. ON LIGHT DLVRY. MODELS

Half-ton De Luxe Panel, $595

Half-ton Standard Panel, $560

1½-ton Panel, $755

Half-ton Standard Canopy Express, $560

Half-ton Standard Canopy Express with Screen Sides, $579

With High Racks, $855

With Tip-Top, $820

1½-ton Combination Farm Body

BB (½ TON) 109" WB

Half-ton Closed Cab Pick-up, $470

Half-ton Closed Cab Pick-up with Canopy Top, $500

Half-ton Special Canopy Express, $580

Half-ton Special Panel, $580

Half-ton Open Cab Pick-up with Canopy Top, $470

MODELS AS OF 3-32

CHASSIS PRICED AS LOW AS $355

32

"CONFEDERATE"

NA, NB, NC, ND (1½ TON) 131" and 157" WB)

1½-ton 131" Open Express, $695

1½-ton 131" Stake Express, $710

1½-ton 157" Stake, $785

1½-ton 157" Van Panel, $1020

1½-ton 131" Platform, $670

RADIATOR STYLE LIKE 1931 CHEV. CARS.

1½-ton 131" High and Wide Express, $705

1½-ton 131" Stake, $700

1½-ton 131" High Rack, $715

DE LUXE ½ TON PANEL = $595.

Sedan Delivery...... $545

NO TRICKS — Camel just costlier tobaccos

The Chevrolet 1½-Ton Panel $715

The Chevrolet 131" Stake.... $655

The Chevrolet 1½-Ton Open Express... $650

The Chevrolet Dump Truck. $815

HOOD DOORS on SOME '32 SEDAN DELIVERYS

RADIATOR STYLE LIKE 1932 CHEV. CARS.

33

"EAGLE" and "MASTER"

CB, OA, OB, OC, OD MODELS

FINAL YEAR FOR '31-STYLE LOUVRES

OLD-STYLE CABS ON PICKUPS and LG. TRUCKS THROUGH '33.

The Chevrolet Closed Cab Pick-Up........ $440

new 206 CID (THROUGH '36)

The Chevrolet ½-Ton Panel $530

116

CHEVROLET

Sedan Delivery, $515
(107" Wheelbase)

Half-Ton Pick-Up with Canopy, $495
(112" Wheelbase)

Half-Ton Canopy Express, $555
(112" Wheelbase)

"EB" MODELS

Half-Ton Panel, $560
(112" Wheelbase)

"QB"
*1½-Ton Platform, $630
(131" Wheelbase)

Half-Ton Pick-Up, $465
(112" Wheelbase)

"QD"
*1½-Ton Chassis and Cab, $605
(157" Wheelbase)

*1½-Ton Chassis, $485
(131" Wheelbase)

*1½-Ton Stake, $660
(131" Wheelbase)

IMPROVED BRAKING ON '35 MODELS

"QA"
1½-Ton Open Express, $655
(131" Wheelbase)

"QD"
*1½-Ton Stake, $720
(157" Wheelbase)

*1½-Ton High Rack, $745
(157" Wheelbase)

(1935 PRICES SHOWN)

NO MORE NAMES FOR YEAR MODELS.

34-35

'35 MODELS: EB, QA, QB, QC, QD

'34 MODELS: DB, PA, PB, PC, PD

COMMERCIAL	½ TON	112" WB	4.11 GR	(107" WB also)
UTILITY	1½	131	5.43	
"	1½	157	"	

CLOSER VIEW OF CANOPY EXPRESS ('34)

ROWELL WOODS GROCERY

"BLUE FLAME" ENGINE
207 CID   70 HP @ 3200 RPM
CARTER CARB.

TIRE SIZES
5.50 × 17   (½ TON)
30 × 5 (FRONT) 32 × 6 (REAR)
(6.00 × 20)   (1½ TON)

"CARRYALL" METAL-BODY WAGON AVAIL. IN 1935.

EARLY '36 CAB STYLE

CHEVROLET

new INSTRUMENT PANEL SIMILAR TO THAT IN 1936 CHEV. "MASTER" SERIES CAR (THROUGH '39.)

HYDRAULIC BRAKES ON ALL BUT EARLY 1½-TON "R."

36

new HORIZONTAL HOOD LOUVRES

SCREENSIDE CANOPY TRUCK

GEAR RATIOS
4.11 (½ TON)
5.43 - 6.17 (1½ TON)

LATER '36 CAB STYLE

PANEL DELIVERY

½ TON : "FB" MODEL (112" WB)
1½ TON MODELS :
RA (131" WB)
RB (131" WB, DUAL REAR WHEELS)
RC (157" WB)
RD (157" WB, DUAL REAR WHEELS)

LATE '36 1½-TON PICKUP has STEEL ARTILLERY WHEELS.

10,110 POUNDS PAY LOAD
AAA
CERTIFIED WEIGHT
SAFE DRIVING ROAD TEST
CHEVROLET MOTOR CO. DETROIT, MICH.

HEAVY-DUTY

FB LIGHT-DUTY ½-TON PICKUP

SEDAN DELIVERY HAS GRILLE LIKE 1936 CHEVROLET CAR.

NEW 216 C.I.D. ENGINE

37 CHEVROLET

78 HP @ 3200 RPM

PICKUP

CHEVROLET

PERFECTED HYDRAULIC BRAKES — NEW HIGH-COMPRESSION VALVE-IN-HEAD ENGINE — MORE LOAD SPACE — IMPROVED LOAD DISTRIBUTION — NEW STEELSTREAM STYLING — IMPROVED FULL-FLOATING REAR AXLE WITH NEW ONE-PIECE HOUSING (on 1½-Ton Models) — NEW ALL-STEEL CAB — PRESSURE STREAM LUBRICATION

UP GOES POWER
DOWN COME COSTS

6.00 × 16 and 7.50 × 15 TIRES LISTED FOR ½ TON TYPES.

GD ¾-TON MODELS RE-INTRODUCED IN MID-SEASON.

SEDAN DELIVERY NOW HAS SPARE TIRE UNDER REAR FLOOR, INSTEAD OF IN FENDER WELL AS BEFORE.

½ TON MODEL IS "GC" (112" WB) (4.11-3.82 GRs)
1½ TON MODELS = MASTER SA, MASTER SB,
   MASTER SP. SB (131" WB)
MASTER SC, MASTER S.D,
MASTER SP. SD (157" WB)
   (5.43-6.17 GRs ON
   1½ TON)

GE IS NEW
1-TON MODEL
(122¼" WB, LIKE ¾ TON)

INTER-CITY S-4

HEAVY-DUTY 1½-TON (NOTE CLEARANCE LIGHTS ON CAB ROOF.)

INTER-CITY TRUCKING SERVICE INC.
GR. WT. 4250

119

IMPROVED DIAPHRAGM-
SPRING CLUTCH,
VOLTAGE-
REGULATOR
GENERATOR

1/2 TON
PICKUP

CHEVROLET

C.O.E.
(RARE)

CAB
('38)

HC,
HD,
HE,
TA, TB,
TC, TD
MODELS

38

1 1/2-TON
STAKE

new TRUCK GRILLE with HEAVIER
HORIZONTAL
MEMBERS

39

JC (1/2 TON ;)
JD (3/4 TON ;)
JE (1 TON ;)
VA, VB, VC, VD (1 1/2 TON ;)
VE, VF, VG, VH, VM,
VN (1 1/2 TON C.O.E.)

78 HP @ 3200 RPM
113 1/2" WB and up

New Chevrolet-Built
CAB-OVER-ENGINE
MODELS

45 MODELS, 8 WHEELBASES
IN 1939.

new V-WINDSHIELD
ON ALL 1939 MODELS.

UNLIKE
PANEL TRUCK,
SEDAN
DELIVERY
IS STYLED LIKE
CHEVROLET
CAR.

TOP PIECE OF GRILLE IS VERT. WIDENED

new HYPOID REAR AXLE

FULL-FLOATING REAR AXLE ON HEAVY-DUTY MODELS with VACUUM-POWER BRAKES and 2-SPEED REAR AXLE OPTIONS.

40

new —
SEALED-BEAM HEADLIGHTS, and PARKING LIGHTS ON FENDERS.

new 4.55 GR ON ¾ TON and 1-TON

C.O.E.
(LOGGER)

MODELS : KC (½ TON;) KD, KE (¾ TON;) KF (1 TON)

KP (½-TON PARCEL DELIV.;)*
WA, WB (1½ TON;)
WD, WE,
WF (1½ TON C.O.E.)

* = SPRING INTRODUCTION

(1940 CHEVROLET CAR-TYPE INSTRUMENT PANEL REPLACES 1936 TYPE (EXCEPT in SCHOOLBUS and FLAT-FACE COWL TYPE.)

BEFORE WORLD WAR II, ALL GM-BUILT TRUCKS OVER 1½-TON CAP'Y. SOLD UNDER GMC NAME.

"WC" IS 1½-TON SCHOOL BUS CHASSIS.

HEAVY-DUTY DUMP TRUCK

new 90-H.P. and 93-H.P. ENGINES ('41)

CHEVROLET
41-47

60 MODELS,
9 WHEELBASES ('41)
(SOME MODELS
ARE
LISTED
BELOW.)

WARTIME
MODELS
HAVE
LESS CHROME
and
NO
FLOOR MAT.

PICKUP

216 OR
new
235 CID,
STARTING
1941.

1941 MODELS : AK, AJ (115" WB;) AL (125" WB;)
AN, YR (134" WB;) YS (160" WB)
C.O.E.s = YU, YV, YW
1942 MODELS : BK, BJ (115" WB;) BL (125" WB;)
(CONT'D. TO '45) BN, MR (134" WB;) MS (160" WB)
C.O.E.s = MU, MV
1946 MODELS : CK (115" WB;) OR, OE (134" WB;)
(INTRO. '45) OS, OF (160" WB)
C.O.E.s = OH, OI, OJ
1947 MODELS : DP (115" WB;) DR (125" WB;) DS, PJ, PV(S,)
(134" WB;) PK, PW(S)(160" WB)
C.O.E.s = PP,
PR, PS   TANKER (C.O.E.)

MILITARY
TRUCKS   ('43)

2-TON
MODELS AVAIL. IN 1946.

VARIETY OF MODELS ILLUSTRATED ('45)

CHEVROLET

Advance-Design

(TOTALLY RESTYLED)

INTRO. SUMMER, 1947

STAKE

PICKUP

('51)

('48)

90 OR 93 HP IN 1948

HP INCREASED TO
92, 102, 105 IN 1950.

92, 107, 108 HP IN 1953.

48-53

YEAR DETERMINED
BY FIRST LETTER IN
MODEL DESIGNATION :

E, Q = 1948
G, S = 1949
H, T = 1950
J, U = 1951
K, V = 1952

WIDE VARIETY OF
ALPHABETICAL SINGLE-
LETTER MODEL
DESIGNATIONS IN 1953.

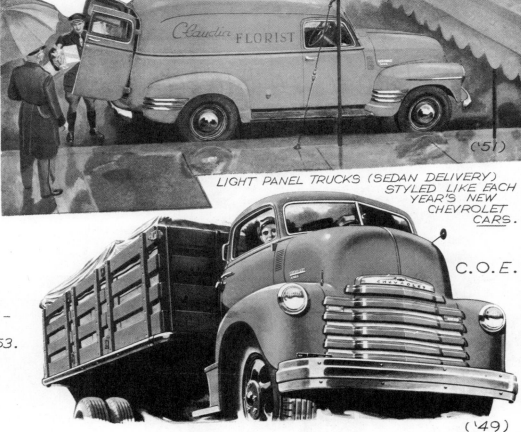

HEAVY PANEL

Claudia FLORIST

('51)

LIGHT PANEL TRUCKS (SEDAN DELIVERY)
STYLED LIKE EACH
YEAR'S NEW
CHEVROLET
CARS.

C.O.E.

('49)

CHEVROLET

DRIVER'S COMPARTMENT OF PANEL TRUCK

THREE 6-CYL. ENGINES : "THRIFTMASTER 235," "LOADMASTER 235," OR "JOBMASTER 261"

54

FIRST RESTYLING SINCE '48.

CAB INTERIOR OF CAB-OVER-ENGINE

NEW 1-PC. CURVED WINDSH.
NEW GRILLE

55-
56

NEW 12-VOLT IGNITION

CHOICE OF 6-CYL. OR NEW V8 ENGINES

NEW "CAMEO" SPT. PICKUP has BROAD FIBERGLASS BOX (THROUGH '57.)

TUBELESS TIRES ON 1/2-TON

CAB-FORWARD

('56)

124

"CAMEO"

CHEVROLET

57

"CAMEO"

LONG-W.B.

"3204" LT. DUTY PICKUP

Flamingo

STEP-VAN

NEW "FLEETSIDE" REPLACES "CAMEO."

"CAMEO CARRIER" NAME USED.

new LT.-DUTY "APACHE" →

"TASK FORCE" SERIES

58

ALSO NEW MEDIUM-DUTY "VIKING 60" and HEAVY-DUTY "SPARTAN 90." ALSO "100" SERIES.

PROD.: 278,632

FOUR HEADLIGHTS (new)

PROD.: 326,102

'59 DASH AND INTERIOR SIMILAR TO '58 MODEL. →

CHEVROLET

1959

59

"FLEETSIDE" PICKUP

EL CAMINO
BY CHEVROLET

INTRODUCED 1959 MODEL YEAR.

119" WHEELBASE (THROUGH '60.)

59

235.5 CID, 135 HP 6-CYL. OR V8 ENGINE with 185 HP, * 283 CID (* THROUGH '67)

OFFICIAL DATE SET FOR EL CAMINO INTRODUCTION: THURSDAY, OCT. 16, 1958.

RIBBED-STEEL LOAD PLATFORM.

4 CHOICES OF TRANSMISSIONS, INCLUDING OPTIONAL TURBOGLIDE.

7.50 × 14 TIRES

283 CID V-8 LISTED AT ONLY 170 HP IN 1960.

60

(PRODUCTION TEMPORARILY SUSPENDED.)

PANEL DELIVERY

CHEVROLET

CARRYALL

Spartan Models

235 - C.I.D. "THRIFT-MASTER" 6 (OTHER 6 and V8 engines also.)

60

FLEETSIDE

STEPSIDE

CHEVROLET 1960

(ADDITIONAL DETAILS NEXT PAGE)

PICKUP CAB

STEP-VAN

new INDEPENDENT FRONT SUSPENSION *with* TORSION BARS *and* BALL JOINTS IN FRONT, COIL SPRINGS AT REAR (ON TRUCKS to 3/4 TON CAP.)

CHEVROLET

60

(CONT'D.)

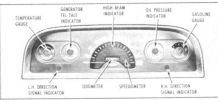

TEMPERATURE GAUGE	GENERATOR TEL-TALE INDICATOR	HIGH BEAM INDICATOR	OIL PRESSURE INDICATOR	GASOLINE GAUGE
L.H. DIRECTION SIGNAL INDICATOR	ODOMETER	SPEEDOMETER	R.H. DIRECTION SIGNAL INDICATOR	

INSTRUMENTS (IN TRUCKS UP TO 2-TON CAP'Y.)

new "TILT-CAB" MODEL

STURDI-BILT TRUCKS CHEVROLET

Rotary Valve Power Steering

AVAIL. ON 60, 70 *and* 80 SERIES

128

PROD. : 394,017

1961 ENGINE SPECS.

TURBO-AIR	6 CYL. 145 CID	80 HP @ 4400 RPM
THRIFTMASTER	6	236	135 @ 4000
JOBMASTER (S.P.)	6	261	150 @ 4000
WORKMASTER (S.P.) V8		348	185-230 HP

FRONT END DETAILS →

TRAVELEZE

MODEL C3604 STEPSIDE PICKUP

61

ENGINES → 6   V8

PICKUP CAB →

MODEL C1434 FLEETSIDE PICKUP

(WIDTHS EXAGGERATED)

60 SERIES (Middleweight)

70 SERIES

PROD. : 342,659

129

AIR - COOLED
REAR-ENGINE
6 CYLS.

CORVAIR

(TRUCKS — 1961 - 1964)
BY CHEVROLET DIVISION OF
G. M.

80 H.P.

8 TO I COMPR.

"CORVAN"
PANEL
TRUCK

61-64

(CORVAIR CARS
PRODUCED
1960-1969.)

"GREENBRIER"
SPORTS WAGON

CORVAIR 95'S
(95" WHEELBASE)

('61)

"RAMPSIDE"
PICKUP
("LOADSIDE" MODEL
DOES NOT
HAVE SIDE
RAMP.)

1 ST DIGIT
IN SERIAL
NUMBER
DETERMINES
YEAR :

"1-R124" ('61)
"2-R124" ('62)
"3-R124" ('63)
ETC.

('64)

CAB ('61)

ADDITIONAL VIEWS OF UNIQUE "RAMPSIDE"

CHEVROLET

DASH LITTLE CHANGED SINCE 1960

235 CID 6,
261 CID 6,
283 CID V8
IN LIGHT-DUTY TRUCKS.

PICKUP

REAR
DETAILS

PICKUP
CAMPER

62

PICKUPS
RESTYLED

A RETURN TO
ONLY 2
HEADLIGHTS

60 SERIES

JOBMASTER

PROD. : 396,940 **131**

CHEVROLET
PICKUP

PROD.: 483,158

NEW HICH-TORQUE 230 CID and 292 CID 6-CYL. ENGINES. NEW LADDER-TYPE FRAMES IN LIGHT-DUTY MODELS.

63

"STEPSIDE"

64

MEDIUM CONV.

6 OR V8, UP TO

FLEETSIDE

409 V8 GAS

LARGER CAB DOORS

V6 DIESEL AVAIL.

WALK-IN STEP-VANS (38 TYPES)

MEDIUM CONVENTIONAL

PROD.: 523,791

CARRYALL (4-W-D. AVAIL.)

new CHEVY-VAN

90-HP 4, OR 120-HP 6

½-TON PANEL (1-TON also)

(RE-INTRODUCED IN *new* CHEVELLE SERIES.)

64

EL CAMINO

"300" OR "MALIBU"

new 115" WB

120 HP 6 CYL. STANDARD

(250-H.P. V8 OPTIONAL)
(2 V8s AVAIL.)
7.00 × 14 TIRES

(BUCKET SEATS, CARPETING, and 4-SPEED TRANS. are OPTIONAL, as are AIR COND. and POWER WINDOWS.)

TRANSISTORIZED RADIO and TINTED GLASS AVAIL.

7.35 × 14 TIRES

SIMUL. WIRE WH. and AM-FM RADIO AVAILABLE.

65

"HI-THRIFT" 194 CID 6 OR "TURBO-FIRE" 283 CID V8 are STANDARD. V8s to 327 CID are OPTIONAL. 3-SPEED, 4-SPEED, O.D. OR POWERGLIDE TRANS.

"STD." OR "CUST."

'66 "CUSTOM" INTERIOR

FRONT END OF SS PASS. MODEL ILLUSTR.

66

133

CHOICE OF 18 LIGHT-DUTY, 258 MEDIUM and HEAVY-DUTY MODELS IN 1965!

HEAVY-DUTY STYLING UNCHANGED

STAKE

CHEVROLET

PROD.: 619,690

65

4, 6, and V8 GAS ENGINES, (also FOUR DIESELS.)

VARIOUS OTHER 1965 TYPES ILLUSTRATED BELOW

SEEN FROM FRONT TO REAR:

CHEVY-VAN, STEP-VAN 7, 60 SERIES TRUCK with VAN BODY, 80 SERIES DIESEL TRACTOR

(½-TON PANEL ACROSS THE STREET.)

CHEVROLET

66

NEW LT.-DUTY 250 CID 6

UP TO 327 CID V8 IN 1/2-TON.

MEDIUM

PICKUP

PROD.: 621,354

NEW SERIES 70000 and 80000 LARGE MODELS with NEW V-6 GAS ENGINES to 478 CID, also V6 and V8 DIESELS to 637 CID.

PROD.: 549,665

ALL-STEEL PICKUP BOX with NEW 1-HAND TAILGATE LATCH

67

CHEVY-VAN 90" or 108" WB

new FENDER SKIRTING

BUCKET SEATS IN "CST" MODELS.

PICKUP and DASH

SIMILAR TO '67, BUT has new SIDE LIGHTS.

68

155-H.P. "250" 6, 170-H.P. "292" 6, NEW 200-H.P. "307" V8, also "327" and "396" (310-H.P.)V8.

NEW SIDE SAFETY LIGHTS on FRONT FENDER PANELS

PROD.: 680,931

new 350 CID V8 (200 or 250 H.P.) IN "40" and "50."

PROD.: 684,748

69

UP TO 8 1/2' BOX AVAIL. IN "FLEETSIDE"

new ALUMINUM GRILLE. IMPROVED SEATS.

PROD.: 492,601

70

FROM 115" W.B.

155-H.P., 250 CID SIX or 200-H.P., 307 CID V-8, plus 3 OTHER ENGINE OPTIONS.

UP TO 310 H.P. IN "400" V-8.

EL CAMINO

67

STD. 230 CID 6 (140 HP)
" 283 CID V8 (195 HP)

(1967 CHEVELLE PASSENGER MODEL ILLUS.)

68

new 116" WB

230 OR 250 CID 6, OR 307, 327 OR 396 CID V8s.

DASH

69

1970: CHOICE OF 250 CID 6 (155 HP @ 4200 RPM) OR V8s OF 307, 350, 400, OR SS-396 CID (200 TO 350 HP RANGE.)

new GRILLE

STD.

REAR STD.

New instrument panel redesigned for appearance and convenience.

70

SS-396 MODEL

"SS" DASH has CIRCULAR GAUGES

SS 396 TAIL

136